EV 3.00

PIPE FITTINGS

 NIPPLES

 PIPE LENGTHS UP TO 22 FT.

 STRAIGHT COUPLING

REDUCING COUPLING

COUPLING

NUT

CAP

STRAIGHT TEE

REDUCING TEE

STREET TEE

STRAIGHT CROSS

REDUCING CROSS

 90° ELBOW

 90° ELBOW

90° ELBOW

45° ELBOW

REDUCING ELBOW

90° STREET ELBOW

45° STREET ELBOW

45° Y-BEND

 REDUCING TEE

REDUCER

UNION (3 PARTS)

PLUG

BUSHING

CAP

RETURN BEND

 PLUG

 45° ELBOW

 TEE

90°

45°

UNION ELBOWS

STREET

UNION TEES

MEASURES OF CAPACITY

1 cup = 8 fl oz
2 cups = 1 pint
2 pints = 1 quart
4 quarts = 1 gallon
2 gallons = 1 peck
4 pecks = 1 bushel

	STANDARD STEEL PIPE ((All Dimensions in inches)				
Nominal Size	Outside Diameter	Inside Diameter	Nominal Size	Outside Diameter	Inside Diameter
1/8	0.405	0.269	1	1.315	1.049
1/4	0.540	0.364	1 1/4	1.660	1.380
3/8	0.675	0.493	1 1/2	1.900	1.610
1/2	0.840	0.622	2	2.375	2.067
3/4	1.050	0.824	2 1/2	2.875	2.469

WOOD SCREWS

LENGTH	GAUGE NUMBERS													
1/4 INCH	0	1	2	3										
3/8 INCH			2	3	4	5	6	7						
1/2 INCH			2	3	4	5	6	7	8					
5/8 INCH				3	4	5	6	7	8	9	10			
3/4 INCH					4	5	6	7	8	9	10	11		
7/8 INCH							6	7	8	9	10	11	12	
1 INCH							6	7	8	9	10	11	12	14
1 1/4 INCH								7	8	9	10	11	12	14	16
1 1/2 INCH							6	7	8	9	10	11	12	14	16	18
1 3/4 INCH									8	9	10	11	12	14	16	18	20
2 INCH									8	9	10	11	12	14	16	18	20
2 1/4 INCH										9	10	11	12	14	16	18	20
2 1/2 INCH													12	14	16	18	20
2 3/4 INCH														14	16	18	20
3 INCH															16	18	20
3 1/2 INCH																18	20	24
4 INCH																18	20	24

WHEN YOU BUY SCREWS, SPECIFY (1) LENGTH, (2) GAUGE NUMBER, (3) TYPE OF HEAD—FLAT, ROUND, OR OVAL, (4) MATERIAL—STEEL, BRASS, BRONZE, ETC., (5) FINISH—BRIGHT, STEEL BLUED, CADMIUM, NICKEL, OR CHROMIUM PLATED.

Popular Mechanics

do-it-yourself encyclopedia

The complete, illustrated home reference guide from the world's most authoritative source for today's how-to-do-it information.

Volume 11

FURNACES

to

GUNS

HEARST DIRECT BOOKS

NEW YORK

Acknowledgements

The Popular Mechanics Encyclopedia is published with the consent and cooperation of POPULAR MECHANICS Magazine.

For POPULAR MECHANICS Magazine:

Editor-in-Chief: *Joe Oldham*
Managing Editor: *Bill Hartford*
Special Features Editor: *Sheldon M. Gallager*
Automotive Editor: *Wade A. Hoyt, SAE*
Home and Shop Editor: *Steve Willson*
Electronics Editor: *Stephen A. Booth*
Boating, Outdoors and Travel Editor: *Timothy H. Cole*
Science Editor: *Dennis Eskow*

Popular Mechanics Encyclopedia

Project Director: *Boyd Griffin*
Manufacturing: *Ron Schoenfeld*
Assistant Editors: *Cynthia W. Lockhart Peter McCann, Rosanna Petruccio*
Production Coordinator: *Peter McCann*

The staff of Popular Mechanics Encyclopedia is grateful to the following individuals and organizations:
Editor: *C. Edward Cavert*
Editor Emeritus: *Clifford B. Hicks*
Production: *Layla Productions*
Production Director: *Lori Stein*
Book Design: *The Bentwood Studio*
Art Director: *Jos. Trautwein*
Design Consultant: *Suzanne Bennett & Associates*
Illustrations: *AP Graphics, Evelyne Johnson Associates, Popular Mechanics Magazine, Vantage Art.*

Contributing Writers: Tony Assenza, *Increase your garage storage space*, page 1342; Rosario Capotosto, *Colonial chair in solid cherry*, page 1298; James Dwyer and John Albert, *Grow a vegetable bonanza in a small plot*, page 1370; Derek Fell, *Bountiful harvest with little work*, page 1368; Bill Fifer and Walter Lange, *Chess set fit for a king*, page 1326; John Gaynor and Harry Wicks, *Greenhouse in your window*, page 1386; Don Geary, *Gardens and gardening*, page 1348; Glenn Hensley, *Keep varmints out of your vegetable patch*, page 1363; Harry Hobbs, *Flip-flop table for backgammon and chess*, page 1318; Stephen J. Howard, *Garage door maintenance*, page 1344; Stephen J. Howard and Roger Hammer, *Furnace failure troubleshooting*, page 1284; George M. Kaler, *Tabletop hockey game you can build*, page 1324; Angus Laidlaw, *The best old guns are new*, page 1402; Wayne C. Leckey, *Portable electric grill you can build*, page 1388; *Colonial dry sink*, page 1294; Mike McClintock, *Greenhouse you can add to your house*, page 1378; Joseph R. Provey, *Multifuel boiler can help you save*, page 1288; *Hotbed extends your growing season*, page 1357; Elmer E. Scott, *Everything's ready when it's time for bridge*, page 1332; Don Shiner, *Colonial comb box*, page 1307; Willard and Elma Walther, *Skammel stool*, page 1316; Norman Ward, *Ball and paddle caddy*, page 1317; Harry Wicks, *This was once an attached garage*, page 1333.

Picture Credits: Popular Mechanics Encyclopedia is grateful to the following for permission to reprint their photography: Burpee Seed Company, pages 1348, 1349, 1350, 1351, 1352, 1353.

ISBN 0-87851-164-4

Library of Congress 85-81760

10 9 8 7 6 5 4 3 2 1
PRINTED IN THE UNITED STATES OF AMERICA

Contents

Furnace failure troubleshooting

■ IT'S A BITTER, 15-below night and the dawn is hours away—when suddenly you awake and realize the furnace isn't working.

At such times, the chances of getting immediate service are pretty slim. Instead of just shivering while waiting, do some troubleshooting yourself. Nine out of ten times, you're likely to find the problem is a minor one you can solve yourself.

Kinds of fuel

Quite often furnace problems are minor ones that you can fix without too much trouble.

Before you start troubleshooting, find out the kind of fuel you use and how dangerous it is. Some fuels are highly explosive, especially if they escape into an enclosed area like a basement.

There are four primary fuel sources (in order of widest use): natural gas, oil, liquefied-petroleum (LP) gas and coal. Coal isn't used much any more.

Oil is relatively safe because it is delivered in liquid form and is vaporized (misted into the air) only at the time of combustion in the furnace.

Natural gas and LP-gas are airborne fuels. Both are potentially explosive and must be carefully regulated in the combustion process.

On call for heat from the thermostat, a furnace control valve senses if a pilot (standing or electronic) is lit. If the pilot is lit, the control opens the main fuel valve to let fuel into the furnace combustion chamber, where the fuel is burned, creating heat for the house.

LP-gas is a more dangerous fuel because it is heavier than air. If it escapes, it will accumulate—or settle—filling a basement like water in a tub. The only way to get it out is to pull it out with special vacuum-type hoses that either your service company or the fire department has.

WARNING: In recent years, there have been serious explosions due to gas-inlet safety valves that have failed "operational" instead of failing "safe." The valve is supposed to sense when a pilot is not lit and not allow a flow of fuel from the main gas line. A defective control can leave the valve open when the pilot is not lit.

If you have any concern about a faulty valve, take these simple precautionary steps:

• Evacuate your home.

• Call either the fire department or your service company from a neighbor's house.

• **Do NOT turn (off or on) any electrical light or other switch**—the spark from flipping a switch (on or off) can ignite a gas leak.

• Use a flashlight (**never a match!**) to find the main valve and turn off the flow of gas.

This same potentially defective control may be on some natural gas furnaces and water heaters. The danger is only slightly less with natural gas than with LP-gas because natural gas is lighter than air. In time, natural gas will be exhausted (up the chimney or flue or into the house so it is "diluted" in the air). LP-gas, on the other hand, settles from the lowest-level floor or basement up.

Even with natural gas, there is a potential for explosion because the natural gas is coming in through the main valve under pressure than it is being exhausted (by convection up the flue).

Two parts of any furnace

Most heating systems consist of two sections. One is the burner portion, where either gas or oil is burned to create heat. The other section delivers the heat to the rooms. Regardless of whether you have an oil or gas burner, the delivery will be made by hot water, steam or forced air. Your first checks should be concerned with the source of heat, the burner.

Checking an oil burner

If trouble hits your oil-fired furnace, try the following:

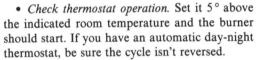

A BROKEN COUPLING in a circulator often can be repaired temporarily by wiring the parts together.

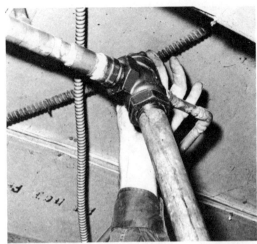

THE FLOW VALVE, usually hidden in a corner, can be opened to feed hot water through the system by gravity.

• *Check thermostat operation.* Set it 5° above the indicated room temperature and the burner should start. If you have an automatic day-night thermostat, be sure the cycle isn't reversed.

Open the thermostat cover. A mercury dial control is sealed and seldom gives trouble. But if you have a contact-point control, dirt on the points could prevent operation. Just pass a new dollar bill or business card between the points to clean them.

• *Check all emergency switches.* Someone may have turned off one accidentally.

Most oil burners have two switches: One is usually on the burner; the other is often at a distant location, such as near the head of the basement stairway or above the basement door leading to the yard. Know where these switches are and make sure they are turned on.

• *Check the two safety switches.* The overload and the stack control relay prevent damage if a problem develops in the electrical circuit.

The overload switch (usually painted red) is on the motor housing. Press it once only. If the motor doesn't start, activate the stack control relay (on the smoke pipe or burner house) once only. Don't fool with these switches if the burner doesn't start.

If you press the stack control relay and the furnace goes on and then off in about 30 seconds, clean the face of the photoelectric cell.

• *Check the fuse or circuit breaker.* Vibration can loosen a fuse, so make certain that it's tight.

If the fuse keeps blowing or a circuit breaker trips repeatedly, there's a malfunction in the electrical system. This requires a service call by a professional.

• *Check the oil valve.* Another malfunction in a late-model oil-burning furnace can be a delayed oil valve that's dirt-clogged or electrically faulty. You *can* run the burner without it in a pinch. Disconnect both input and output oil lines on the valve and remove the valve. Then connect the input directly to the output line. This should be only a temporary fix until you can get the unit serviced.

• *Check oil supply.* Gauges on indoor tanks can stick, showing an oil reserve when there is none. Tap the gauge. If the cap of an outside tank is accessible, take a dipstick reading.

• *Check the nozzle.* Finally, the malfunction

IF AN OIL BURNER FAILS, locate the overload switch (usually found on the motor housing) and press.

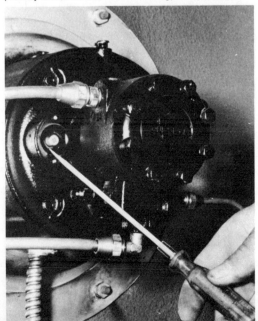

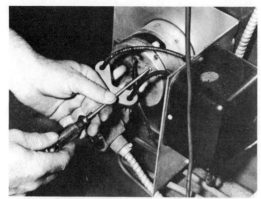

AN OIL BURNER may be controlled by a photoelectric cell. Just remove the small screw to gain access.

THE STACK CONTROL RELAY is usually located on the smoke pipe or burner housing. Press it only once.

could be in the oil nozzle-and-electrode assembly inside the burner. Check them out first, but first be sure to turn off all emergency switches. **Never work inside the burner with the switches turned on.**

Remove the access plate, or unscrew and drop the transformer so you can reach the inside of the burner. Loosen the oil line connection with a wrench and disconnect the transformer and electrode wires. These are usually held by snap-on connectors. Take the electrode-nozzle assembly out of the burner, being careful not to change the setting of the electrodes.

Unscrew the nozzle. You'll find a filter inside. Unscrew that and wash it in warm water. (It could be clogged and blocking oil flow.) You'll find a small setscrew inside the nozzle. Unscrew that, too, and wash it.

Now blow into the nozzle. Air will pass through freely if it is clear and working. If not, you're out of luck unless you have a spare nozzle on hand.

Don't try to open the present nozzle with an

icepick. Probing will widen the hole, upset the fuel ratio and cause the burner to puff. Although this can't harm the system, the burner won't function.

Clean the electrodes carefully, using a rag or fine steel wool. Again, **do not disturb the setting** or puffing will occur. Put everything back together, turn on the emergency switches and press the stack control relay.

If your burner is the rotary type, it won't have a nozzle. Just reach into the burner with a rag and carefully wipe the electrodes clean. Make sure that all emergency switches are *off*.

Checking a gas burner

If you have a gas-fired heating system, find a flashlight—**never light a match or turn an electrical switch (on or off) until you are sure you don't have a gas leak.**

Gas in its basic form is odorless, but suppliers (utilities or jobbers) deliver gas with an odor added so you can smell a gas leak. Your nose is a handy tool!

There are two main gas control points: One is the lever control where gas comes into the house (from a pipeline or the storage tank outside); the other is where the gas line enters the appliance (furnace, water heater, clothes dryer, etc.).

Turning off the main gas line lever will turn out all standing pilots. Turning off the gas control at the appliance will cut off the gas to that appliance and its pilot. Some appliances do not have a pilot but use a spark igniter that lights the burner with an electrical spark.

If you smell gas throughout the house, turn off the main valve lever. If you smell gas at or near a single appliance, turn off the valve at that appliance. If you smell no gas, then begin troubleshooting the furnace as follows:

• *Check controls.* Follow the same routine as shown in the section "Checking an oil burner" for checking the thermostat, fuse or circuit breaker, and boiler, circulator or forced-air delivery systems.

Gas burners have only one electrical switch—if you are certain you have no gas leak, look for this switch on the furnace and turn it on. This gives electrical power to run the furnace fan or blower and also powers the electrical connections of the thermostat with the furnace.

• *Checking the pilot.* Newer furnaces are lit with an energy-saving spark. Older furnaces have a standing pilot or tiny gas flame that stays on all the time. There are instructions on the furnace about relighting it—sometimes it will get blown out by a gust of wind or air in the house. Sometimes the line or outlet at the flame can get clogged with dirt or carbon. If the pilot won't stay lit, shut off the valve controlling the gas to the appliance and then shut off the electrical switch. Tap the pilot burner with a screwdriver or wrench to knock loose a minor clog. Turn the gas valve to "pilot" and try to light it again. Turn on the main valve only when the pilot remains lit. **Do *not* try to light the main burner by hand instead of with the pilot.** The main burner flares up with the surge of gas from the main valve and could seriously burn you if you try to light it by hand.

If the pilot will not remain lit, the appliance is trying to tell you something is wrong. It's time now for a service call from a person with more troubleshooting and repair experience.

If the pilot is lit, then the trouble is elsewhere.

Checking delivery systems

This checklist applies to both oil and gas-fired systems:

• *Steam systems: check the boiler gauge.* The burner will shut off automatically if the water level gets too low. But before refilling a hot boiler, let it cool down to avoid the chance of cracking. The burner should run again when the boiler gauge reaches the half-full mark.

• *Hot-water systems: check the circulator.* One in need of lubrication won't circulate hot water, even though the burner itself will continue to run. Lubricate only with grades of oil or cup grease recommended on the instruction plate found on the circulator body.

If there is a reset button on the circulator, press it once. If there is no button, try giving the unit a slap with your hand.

A circulator will stop heat delivery if it breaks a coupling. Put your ear close to a suspected part and listen for a sharp, rapping sound. To repair a broken coupling temporarily, remove the access cover and wire the broken crosspieces together.

• *Forced-air systems: check for a clogged filter.* This is a major cause of reduced heat. If no spare, remove the filter (there may be more than one), take it outside and knock it against something hard to loosen the dirt. Better yet, go over the filter with the radiator attachment of your vacuum cleaner to pull out much of the dirt.

• *Check the blower motor.* A short is usually indicated by on-off cycling in short spurts or by its refusal to run at all. While waiting for service, however, you *can* get some heat, since the burner is still functioning. Just remove all filters from the furnace. Since hot air rises, some heat will go through the ducts to the registers.

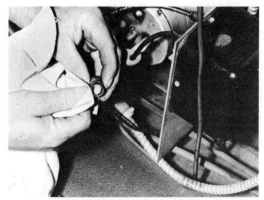

MODERN OIL BURNERS may have a delayed oil valve. In a pinch, remove the valve and connect the lines.

REMOVE THE NOZZLE with two wrenches. Clean the filter and setscrew, test the nozzle and then reassemble.

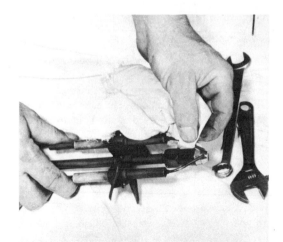

CARBON MAY BE FOULING the electrodes. Wipe them off with either a clean cloth or fine steel wool.

Save with a multifuel boiler

■ THE FIRST TIME you fire up your multifuel boiler with a load of wood, you also take on part of the responsibility for providing heat for your family. In the past, a contract with the oil company always took care of everything. The burner fed itself and deliveries were automatic.

Now you can call the shots—without giving up the admitted convenience of oil. The unit shown here will burn oil, gas, coal, coke or wood and even operate on electricity.

Schedule to complete your installation in the spring, when a service interruption will not be critical and installers are not completely booked.

The payback period for your initial cost can be relatively short. If you use oil to heat domestic water during the mild weather months, you can then use wood for both domestic hot water and space heating during the winter. If you are ambitious and have a source of supply, the wood is available for only your effort in chopping it. If your cost for wood is low, you can pay for the multifuel unit in three or four years.

Planning the installation

Begin planning your installation by looking at available units and sending for manufacturers' literature. After choosing the unit that suits your needs, check the dimensions of access to the basement, condition and size of your chimney flue, and the size of the area where the unit will be installed. Be sure you can get the unit into the basement without removing a wall or floor section. Be sure the chimney is the right size, in good repair and tile-lined. Also be sure there is adequate space for recommended clearances. Only then are you ready to visit the local building department to get a heating permit.

Codes vary from state to state and even from city to city. A few city codes have not approved multifuel units, so check before you buy. Don't chance an illegal installation—it may lower the resale value of your home. And if you should have a fire, the insurance adjuster will be the first person to find out if you had a valid heating permit.

When it comes to actual installation, some distributors encourage homeowners to participate. Depending on the dealer, you can assemble or trim out the unit yourself and save part of the installation cost. Or you can choose to work with a top-notch crew of professional installers and get invaluable knowledge of the unit.

Connecting the electric controls, circulating

INSTALLATION of boiler jacket and mounting of doors and components can be done by the homeowner.

CONNECTING overheat control and master hot-water control normally requires professional help.

BEFORE FLUE pipe was installed, thimble was mortared in place. Then flue pipe was inserted and joint sealed.

AIR PURGER, valves and copper pipes were plumbed and soldered according to the manufacturer's recommendations.

FLUE PIPE sections were fastened with sheet-metal screws to keep them from separating due to vibration.

OIL FEED LINE to burner was protected by slipping an old garden hose over the exposed tubing.

CIRCULATOR PUMP (A) on return line operates constantly during heating season. Auto mix valve (B) feeds more—or less—hot water from boiler to radiators, depending on thermostat's call for heat.

BOILER MAINTENANCE

If you are accustomed to low-maintenance fuels like gas or oil, be aware that alternative fuels (coal and especially wood) will demand more of your attention. Chimneys, for instance, must be cleaned once a year. The stovepipe between the boiler and the chimney must be removed and inspected for corrosion, creosote and soot at least twice during a heating season. The oil or gas burner should be adjusted, and the burner firebox cleaned, once a year. Cleaning of the inside boiler walls and flue passages must be done at least every two months during the heating season. Otherwise, a buildup of creosote will slow heat transfer.

SCOOP IS USED for emptying ashes. They should be removed before they touch grates and restrict airflow.

WIRE FLUE BRUSH and long-handle scraper are provided with unit for cleaning creosote from boiler.

METER reads 23-percent moisture content in logs seasoned 10 months—slightly high for burning.

pump and valves is best left to *licensed* professionals familiar with your unit—unless you are blessed with plenty of time, can acquire a good installation manual and have background in plumbing and electrical work.

Differences and advantages

Since solid-fuel burning is inherently different from burning gas or oil, the heat distribution and safety systems should be more sophisticated than conventional systems. The installation can use a mixing valve and circulator that runs continuously, or it can be a typical hydromic system that periodically circulates fairly high-temperature water. The four-way mixing valve adds more or less return water to the supply being pumped to the radiators and is controlled by the house thermostat. Aside from using more heat more efficiently and eliminating costly short-cycling of the oil burner, other advantages you will obtain through continuous circulation include:
• Longer boiler life due to elimination of thermal shock to the boiler caused by surges of cold return water every time the circulator is started.
• Longer circulator life, since most wear in circulators occurs during motor start-up.
• A quieter house during the heating season.
• A more comfortable house since the heat is more even.

Continuous circulation of water to radiators also acts as a safety feature for a wood-fired hot-water heating system. Since the wood fire is always generating heat (it can't be turned off like an oil burner), the system will dispose of the heat efficiently. In a conventional system, there is a greater possibility of boiler overheat (when there is no circulation) and creosote formation (caused by the fire burning too slowly between sporadic calls for heat).

Other safety features on the unit shown include a high-temperature overheat control that causes overheated boiler water to circulate to radiators, even if there is no call from the house thermostat.

Both the domestic hot-water coil and the boiler have pressure-relief valves piped down to near the floor or to a drain.

A backflow preventer was installed on the feed line of the unit shown to prevent contaminated water in the heat distribution loop from entering the domestic water supply.

In a power failure

Even with the electricity off, the multifuel boiler can keep your house warm. When a power outage occurs, a special solenoid valve opens and lets hot boiler water gravity-feed to the radiators, bypassing the check valve. The fire during such an outage would have to be fueled carefully and in moderation to prevent overheating the boiler. The automatic draft regulator will continue to control the fire even without electricity.

Renewable fuels

The dwindling supplies of oil and gas will inevitably force us to depend on safe, renewable energy sources instead of nonrenewable and species-endangering ones. During the transition, the smart homeowner will leave open as many options as possible—a multifuel boiler or furnace fills the bill.

Sofa bed you can build

■ THIS GUEST BED that doubles as a sofa is basically a couch built around a purchased high-rise (pop-up) trundle-bed frame.

The inner frame is built first, assembled with 2½-in. No. 10 flathead screws and reinforced with 3-in. corner braces. The crosspiece should be offset about 1-in. from center to allow for carriage bolts that will attach the back of the outer frame.

LOWER FLAP DOOR conceals a high-rise trundle bed and lifts for access to it. The lower bed snaps up to the same height as the upper bed.

MATTRESSES butt together at the same level to provide for a full double-bed width. The unit also offers option of being made up and used as two beds.

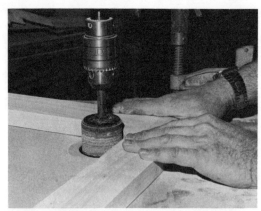

DRUM SANDER attachment in a drill press or a portable electric drill is used to finish off the inside corner blocks after they're glued in place.

ROUT a continuous ¼ x ¼-in. groove spaced ⁷/₁₆ in. from each inside opening. For a good job, use an edge guide that helps you follow inside curves.

DRIVE REED SPLINE into the glued groove with mallet and wedge while cane is wet, taking care to maintain proper alignment of the cane pattern.

TRIM OFF the excess with a razor knife when glue in groove has dried and cane is taut. A liberal allowance of excess cane makes the installation easier.

Web the completed inner frame next and staple No. 40 muslin on top of the webbing.

For the outer frame, cut stiles and rails as shown on the plan, then dowel, glue and clamp all joints to assemble each side of the frame and the back. To make the 40 curved filler blocks for the inside corners, rip a 5/4 board to 4-in. width and draw 10 4-in.-dia. circles just a kerf-width apart on it with a compass. Saw the board apart between the circles, then use a jigsaw or sabre saw to cut out circles. "Waste" around each circle will yield four corner blocks curved to a 2-in. radius. You can cut the circles in half and use these scrap pieces to clamp the glued-in blocks without marring them.

After the frame sides and back have been assembled and sanded, knock down the outward-facing edges of openings with a ⅜-in. rounding-over bit in a router. On opposite sides, rout a ¼x¼-in. continuous groove around each opening, 7/16 in. from its edge. Use an edge guide to follow the curves of the corners—some of this work will be visible when the piece is finished.

Installing cane and splines

Paint or varnish the frames. (The cane can be painted or varnished after installation, but varnish will darken it.) When the finish is completely dry, cut pieces of machine-woven (prewoven or "pressed") cane to fit the openings. Soak cane and reed splines in warm water for about two hours to soften them. Dribble a bead of white glue into the groove around the opening, carefully align the wet cane on it, then hammer in the spline with a mallet and a hardwood wedge. Hang flap door on the front of the unit to complete basic assembly.

Sources: You'll need to find a bed retailer willing to sell just the lower frame. An upholsterers' supply shop should carry webbing and muslin (foam, too).

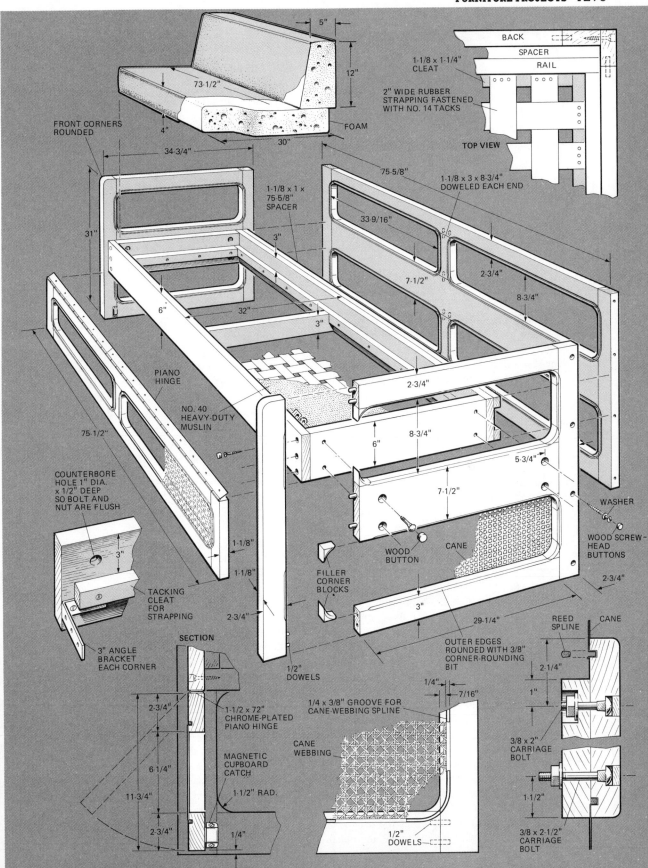

5"

12"

73-1/2"

4"

30"

FOAM

FRONT CORNERS ROUNDED

BACK

SPACER

1-1/8 x 1-1/4" CLEAT

RAIL

2" WIDE RUBBER STRAPPING FASTENED WITH NO. 14 TACKS

TOP VIEW

34-3/4"

1-1/8 x 1 x 75-5/8" SPACER

75-5/8"

1-1/8 x 3 x 8-3/4" DOWELED EACH END

31"

33-9/16"

3"

7-1/2"

2-3/4"

8-3/4"

6"

32"

3"

2-3/4"

PIANO HINGE

NO. 40 HEAVY-DUTY MUSLIN

8-3/4"

5-3/4"

6"

75-1/2"

7-1/2"

WASHER

COUNTERBORE HOLE 1" DIA. x 1/2" DEEP SO BOLT AND NUT ARE FLUSH

1-1/8"

1-1/8"

FILLER CORNER BLOCKS

WOOD BUTTON

CANE

WOOD SCREW-HEAD BUTTONS

2-3/4"

TACKING CLEAT FOR STRAPPING

3"

2-3/4"

1/2" DOWELS

3"

29-1/4"

REED SPLINE

CANE

3" ANGLE BRACKET EACH CORNER

SECTION

2-1/4"

OUTER EDGES ROUNDED WITH 3/8" CORNER-ROUNDING BIT

1"

2-3/4"

1-1/2 x 72" CHROME-PLATED PIANO HINGE

1/4"

7/16"

1/4 x 3/8" GROOVE FOR CANE-WEBBING SPLINE

3/8 x 2" CARRIAGE BOLT

6-1/4"

MAGNETIC CUPBOARD CATCH

CANE WEBBING

11-3/4"

1-1/2" RAD.

1-1/2"

2-3/4"

1/4"

1/2" DOWELS

3/8 x 2-1/2" CARRIAGE BOLT

Colonial dry sink

■ SERVING ORIGINALLY as a place to wash and to store a porcelain water pitcher and bowl, the charming colonial dry sink of yester-year continues to be a graceful and useful piece of furniture some hundred years later.

Today it provides a perfect place to display your indoor plants; it has two roomy drawers felt-lined for silverware and there is ample storage below for linens behind two raised-panel doors.

The little beauty you see here was built from common pine, which you can buy at any lumberyard. Its authentic design makes it a collector's item, and its simple construction makes it a natural for the home craftsman to duplicate.

The ends require pieces which measure 17½ in. wide. Since you can't buy pine this wide, you will have to glue and dowel several 1 x 8 (¾ x 7½ in.) boards together. With the possible exception of the doors, the ends are the only members you will have to build up. The wide pieces for the sink top, shelf, bottom and back are cut from plywood. Both ends are worked as right and left-hand members when you run the dadoes across the inside, cut the rabbets for the plywood back and rip the set-back edges at the front. The latter is done on your table saw to assure a straight cut. Here the work is ripped ¾ in. in from the edge for a distance of 25⅝ in., then backed off and the stopped cut is finished by hand. Notice that the ¼-in.-wide rabbets along the rear edges are made ¾ in. wide for a distance of 7 in. down from the top.

The scroll design at the top of the ends is cut with your sabre saw, then both inside and outside edges are antiqued (distressed) by rounding and sanding.

When you have the sink top and bottom plywood members cut to size, you can glue them in the dadoes of the solid-pine ends. Use long clamps if you have them and check the assembly with a square before setting it aside.

While the glue is drying, make the scroll-cut member for the back. This is cut from a 1 x 10 pine board to rest in the ¾-in. end rabbets previously made and has a rabbet cut along the bottom edge to fit over the sink top. Round and sand the edges of the scroll as you did the ends and then glue and nail the piece in place, driving the nails from the back.

Next, make the framework for the front. This is a separate unit made from ¾-in. pine strips to fit flush with the ends of the cabinet and even with the top surfaces of the sink top and bottom. Butt, dowel and glue the joints; if you have clamps, use them to pull the joints together. When the framework is completed, glue it to the cabinet.

Now you can add the scroll-cut base to the front and ends. Rip a board long enough to make the three pieces, rabbet one edge so it will lap the base and bevel the outer edge as shown. The pieces are mitered at the front and sawed off even at the back. Attach the members with glue and screws from the inside.

A ¼-in. back is added to the cabinet next. Notice that it has "legs" at each side which continue past the sink bottom. The legs provide support for the base members at the rear corners. After the back is glued and nailed in place, add glue blocks to these inside corners.

Now you can make the slanting front piece. It is rabbeted along three edges to lap the front frame and the cabinet ends, and is shorter than the overall length of the cabinet. Cut the top edge as indicated, round the edges as before and glue in place.

The drawers ride on rails installed along each side of the openings. They are cut on the table saw from 2 x 4 stock and rest on a cleat glued and nailed to the cabinet back. The outer rails are glued and screwed to the cabinet sides. The center rails (actually two rails in one) are glued at the front and nailed to the cleat at the back. Notice that the rails project 1/16 in. into the opening on each side. Follow typical drawer construction when you make the drawers and take dimensions directly from the cabinet. The drawer fronts are rabbeted all around so they will lap the openings.

Unless you happen to have a shaper and a set of regular sash cutters, it will be almost impossible for you to duplicate a factory-made raised-panel door in which the panel sits in a groove and the molded, mortised members are undercut to fit perfectly at the corners. The best a home craftsman can do is to assemble simple frames of ¾-in. stock, butt-glue the joints and use a portable router to run the rabbet on the back for the panel and to shape the molded edge on the front. The overall effect is practically the same and few will notice any change. The main difference is that the cutter will leave a rounded inside corner instead of a square one.

Another way to make the doors is to run the stock like picture-frame molding and simply miter the corners. However, this makes a somewhat less authentic-looking door.

The raised panel is a simple thing to run on your table saw by tilting the blade and passing the work through on edge. Then the shallow shoulder cut is made with the work flat on the table and against the fence. A ⅛ x ¾-in. flat molding holds the panel in the frame and covers the joint. As with the drawers, the doors are rabbeted all around so they will lap the openings.

Appropriate hand-wrought hinges should be picked for the doors. You'll need the kind which are offset to accommodate the door lip. White porcelain knobs carry out the colonial feeling.

If you plan to use live potted plants in the sink which require watering and tending, you should fit the top with a shallow sheet-metal tray.

To finish your dry sink, first sand the wood until you are satisfied with its smoothness. You can start with a medium grit and finish with a fine-grit paper. (If you prefer an early American

The rear view shows how the back panel is cut to provide "legs" that support the corner glue blocks

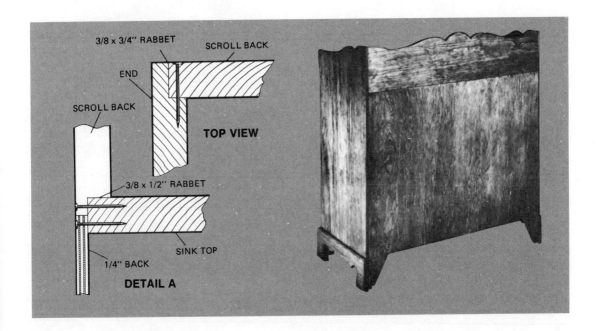

3/8 x 3/4" RABBET

SCROLL BACK

END

SCROLL BACK

TOP VIEW

3/8 x 1/2" RABBET

SINK TOP

1/4" BACK

DETAIL A

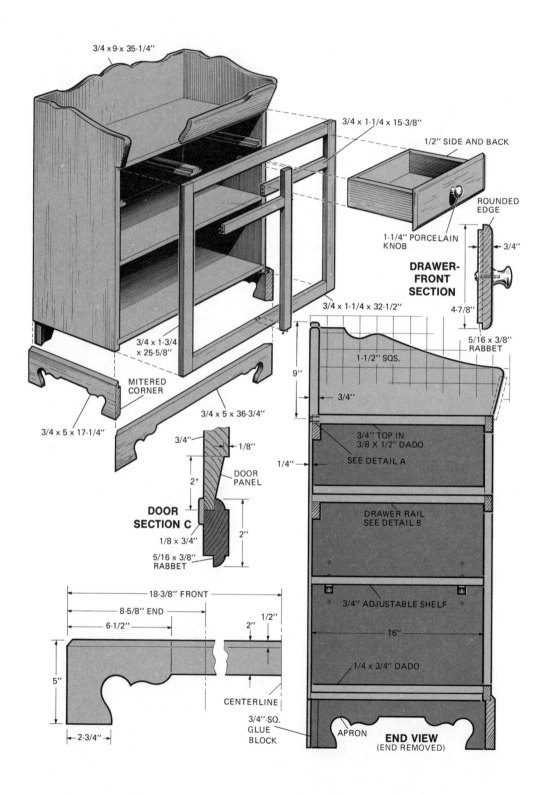

3/4 x 9- x 35-1/4"

3/4 x 1-1/4 x 15-3/8"

1/2" SIDE AND BACK

ROUNDED EDGE

DRAWER-FRONT SECTION

1-1/4" PORCELAIN KNOB

3/4"

4-7/8"

5/16 x 3/8" RABBET

3/4 x 1-1/4 x 32-1/2"

3/4 x 1-3/4 x 25-5/8"

MITERED CORNER

3/4 x 5 x 36-3/4"

3/4 x 5 x 17-1/4"

1-1/2" SQS.

9"

3/4"

3/4" TOP IN 3/8 X 1/2" DADO
SEE DETAIL A

1/4"

DRAWER RAIL SEE DETAIL B

3/4" ADJUSTABLE SHELF

16"

1/4 x 3/4" DADO

3/4"
1/8"

DOOR PANEL

2"

DOOR SECTION C

1/8 x 3/4"

2"

5/16 x 3/8" RABBET

18-3/8" FRONT

8-5/8" END

6-1/2"

1/2"

2"

5"

CENTERLINE

3/4"-SQ. GLUE BLOCK

APRON

END VIEW
(END REMOVED)

2-3/4"

"primitive" look, *don't* oversand the wood.) After the sanding, wipe off all sawdust.

For a natural or stained finish apply the color stain you prefer, following directions on the can label. Allow to set for approximately 15 to 20 minutes and then—using a clean rag—wipe off all excess, rubbing *with* the grain. Allow the piece to dry overnight (24 hours). If desired, the piece can be antiqued by blending in burnt umber with a rag. (This, too, must be allowed to dry for 24 to 48 hours.) To finish, apply two coats of semigloss varnish. Allow 24 hours drying time between coats. After approximately three weeks, rub lightly with double-O steel wool saturated with Butcher's Wax and buff to a sheen.

Antiquing hints: Use burnt umber—direct from the tube—to simulate any surfaces that will be exposed to the most dirt accumulation over a long period of time (in corners or crevices, for example). And always blend the burnt umber into the mating stain so that there is no visible "line" or joint.

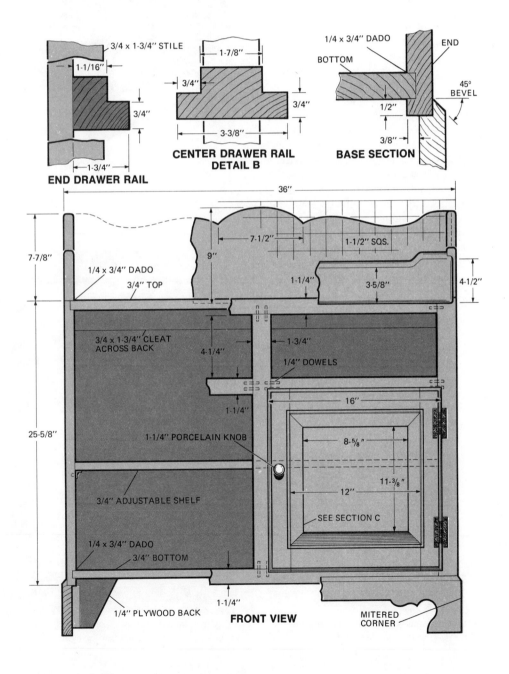

Colonial chair in solid cherry

■ HERE'S A PROJECT to involve you in a number of shop skills, including repeat turnings, spokeshave shaping, lap-jointing and angle drilling. And, since this handsome cherry chair is planned for standard-size, ready-made cushions, you needn't worry about upholstering procedures.

This chair is sturdy, despite its trim lines and somewhat delicate appearance, and its legs, with 1¼-in. tenons, won't loosen in a lifetime. Lumber requirements are minimal: 12 ft. of ⁵/₄ x 8-in. and 8 ft. of ⁸/₄ x 8-in. cherry, plus three lengths of ¾-in. hardwood dowels.

Start with the side panels. Make over-size, rough-cut sections as shown in the diagram. Fit pieces closely to save lumber. It's wise to position sections one atop the other in proper relationship, then lay a full-size paper pattern of the side in place to double check proper angular placement. Remove the pattern and scribe lines to indicate lap-joint limits.

For safety when cutting wide laps, leave a bit uncut at the outside end until all inner portions are cleaned out. This can avoid a nasty accident, such as the workpiece dipping too deeply into the blade.

Make right and left sections for each side for symmetry of joint lines. Glue the pieces, using a few nails in the waste areas to prevent sliding during clamping. Then bandsaw sides to size and

THE LAP JOINT is cleared with a dado blade. Notice the end portion is left as a temporary support.

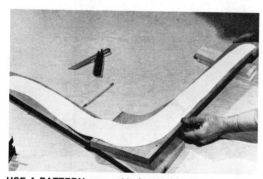

USE A PATTERN as a guide for positioning the side sections before you mark off the lap-joint limits.

A LARGE LAP joint like this is extremely strong. Be sure to reverse the position for left and right sides.

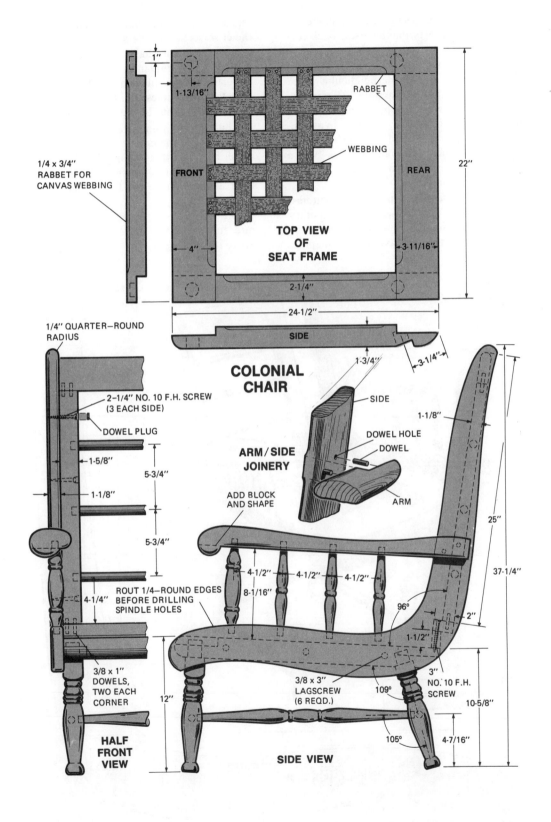

1/4 x 3/4"
RABBET FOR
CANVAS WEBBING

1-13/16"

RABBET

WEBBING

FRONT

REAR

22"

4"

3-11/16"

**TOP VIEW
OF
SEAT FRAME**

2-1/4"

24-1/2"

SIDE

1-3/4"

3-1/4"

**COLONIAL
CHAIR**

SIDE

1/4" QUARTER—ROUND
RADIUS

2-1/4" NO. 10 F.H. SCREW
(3 EACH SIDE)

DOWEL PLUG

1-5/8"

5-3/4"

1-1/8"

5-3/4"

4-1/4"

ROUT 1/4—ROUND EDGES
BEFORE DRILLING
SPINDLE HOLES

3/8 x 1"
DOWELS,
TWO EACH
CORNER

**HALF
FRONT
VIEW**

12"

**ARM / SIDE
JOINERY**

ADD BLOCK
AND SHAPE

DOWEL HOLE

DOWEL

ARM

1-1/8"

25"

37-1/4"

96°

2"

1-1/2"

4-1/2" 4-1/2" 4-1/2"

8-1/16"

3/8 x 3"
LAGSCREW
(6 REQD.)

109°

3"

NO. 10 F.H.
SCREW

105°

4-7/16"

10-5/8"

SIDE VIEW

smooth. When rounding edges, don't shape the juncture of the armrests and the inside back corners.

Due to the bottom curve on side panels, you need a simple jig to bore perpendicular holes accurately for the armrest spindles. Clamp two 2x4 pieces to the work to hold it in the proper plane as indicated in the drawing. Clamp assembly to the drill-press table and bore the holes. Cut armrest pieces and bore spindle holes before contouring the top surface so the pieces will rest flat and true on the table.

After boring the holes in armrest bottoms, screw on a piece of 2 × 4 to serve as a temporary clamping block to hold the work in the vise while you shape it with a spokeshave. Before shaping,

remove some waste with the bandsaw. Note that the cross section of the armrest takes on varying curves. You can shape the pieces by eye but if you need guidance, cut some cardboard templates from a full-size sketch of the contours. Bore the dowel holes after you notch out the back of the armrest, but before cutting any curves.

While the chair legs are angled (in one plane, front to rear), the construction and assembly is novel because of its simplicity. Front legs are driven straight into the seat frame, but achieve their angle because the frame slants down toward the back.

The seat and back frames are made up as separate subassemblies and then joined together. Make the necessary cuts on the seat frame parts

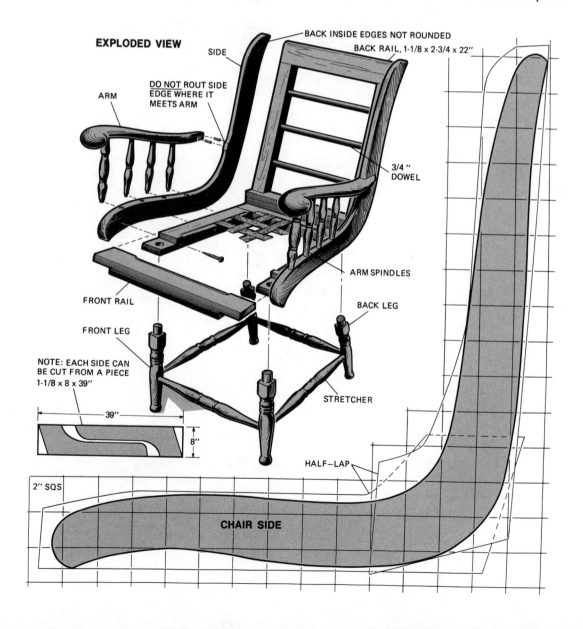

EXPLODED VIEW

BACK INSIDE EDGES NOT ROUNDED
BACK RAIL, 1-1/8 x 2-3/4 x 22"
SIDE
DO NOT ROUT SIDE EDGE WHERE IT MEETS ARM
ARM
3/4" DOWEL
ARM SPINDLES
FRONT RAIL
BACK LEG
FRONT LEG
NOTE: EACH SIDE CAN BE CUT FROM A PIECE 1-1/8 x 8 x 39"
STRETCHER
39"
8"
HALF-LAP
2" SQS
CHAIR SIDE

AN AUXILIARY work-support platform is a handy aid when bandsawing awkwardly shaped pieces like this.

RIPPLES made by the bandsaw blade can be smoothed out with a spokeshave as shown, or a plane and sander.

A ROUTER with a ¼-round bit will cut round edges on the side panels. *Don't* shape where armrest meets panel.

AN ORBITAL finishing sander with high o.p.m. lets you do an excellent smoothing job with little effort.

TO DRILL spindle holes accurately, sandwich the side between two blocks to hold it true and steady.

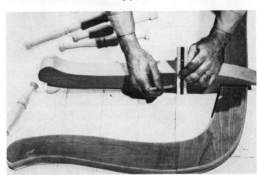

A FULL-SIZE SKETCH offers the easiest way to locate the exact position for holes in the armrests and sides.

AN EXPLODED VIEW shows how the seat frame is made up. This view of the seat is from the top side.

BOTTOM VIEW OF FRAME: Holes are predrilled for illustration. They can be bored after the piece is glued.

A POWER BLOCK PLANE, used to trim the assembled seat frame to the desired size, saves muscles.

THE SEAT FRAME must be propped up when you bore the angled rear holes. *Don't* try this without clamps.

THE BACK FRAME is butt-jointed and doweled. Insert the long dowel spindles before assembling the frame.

THE BACK is joined to the bottom frame with screws and glue. Use a damp cloth to wipe off the excess glue.

before assembly, including the angled notches below and wide rabbets for the webbing on the top side. The broad area of the lap joints supports a lot of glue so you need no doweling here. Besides, the leg tenons serve as huge dowels. Back framing members are butted, so paired dowels are called for at corners.

You'll need a simple jig, consisting of a large plank clamped to the drill-press table, to support the seat frame at the proper angle for boring holes for the rear legs. Round the front end of the seat and the top edge of the back frame, thoroughly sand all the exposed surfaces, then screw and glue the back to the seat. The side panels are glued on next. Use flathead, countersunk screws through the sides of the back frame and ⅜ x 3-in. lag screws to secure the seat framing.

You are now ready for the fun part of the project: turning the spindles. If you do not own a lathe attachment for making duplicate turnings, it will take you a little longer to do the work. The job will take some patience and frequent checking.

Start by making a full-size sketch of each of the turnings for reference. Rip the turning blocks

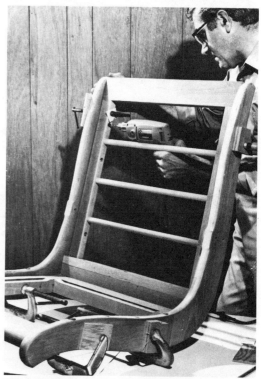

FOR ACCURACY, holes for the screws are drilled on the spot with the members clamped in their final position.

A SPOKESHAVE will let you do a slick carving job on the armrests. The various contours are shown on the following page.

DON'T RUSH the shaping. Use full-size drawings of the contours, plus calipers, to make frequent checks.

for the four legs and the two leading arm spindles out of $^8/_4$-in. stock; the $^5/_4$-in. material will take care of the rest of the spindles. Since the legs have squared ends, you'll have to smooth-finish these blocks. Because you will occasionally have to remove the turnings from the lathe, put a reference mark on one facet of the spur center and mark each block accordingly so that the pieces will always go back on the lathe in their original orientation.

Rough-turn all the blocks into cylinders, except for the leg blocks. These must be turned with squared shoulders not only at the top, but also in the waste area beyond the bottom. This is important because the two flats will later provide the only means of *successfully* drilling the holes for the spindles with *ease* and precision.

To prevent the corners of the square sections from splintering, first make nicking cuts with the toe of the skew. Now you can proceed to make sizing cuts with the parting tool on all of the roughed-in cylinders. It's desirable to keep all diameters a bit oversize to allow for the finishing cuts.

Complete any one of the turnings and then tie it to a shop-made hinging board that's mounted

SHOP-TURNED SPINDLES used in the chair test your duplicate-turning skills, a task that is simplified if you make full-size patterns first. The turnings are even easier if you own a duplicating attachment for your lathe.

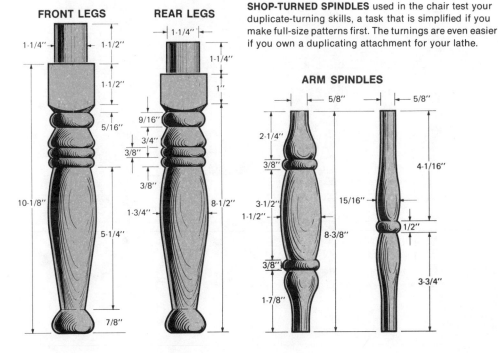

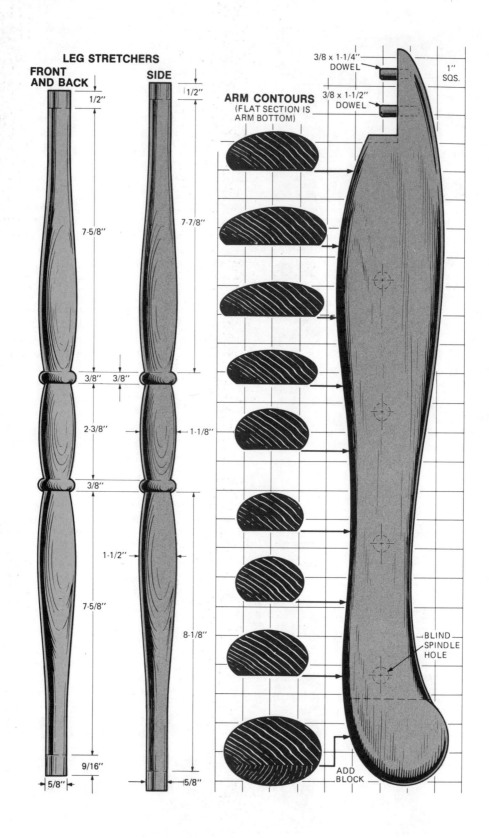

LEG STRETCHERS

FRONT
AND BACK

SIDE

1/2"

1/2"

7-5/8"

7-7/8"

3/8" 3/8"

3/8"

2-3/8"

1-1/8"

3/8"

1-1/2"

7-5/8"

8-1/8"

9/16"

5/8"

5/8"

3/8 x 1-1/4"
DOWEL

3/8 x 1-1/2"
DOWEL

1"
SQS.

ARM CONTOURS
(FLAT SECTION IS
ARM BOTTOM)

BLIND
SPINDLE
HOLE

ADD
BLOCK

A DISC SANDER is the handiest tool for rounding off ball end of the arm. Added block is required here.

THE SIDE and arm must be rigidly clamped precisely in position when you bore the holes for the joint-dowels.

THE MASTER SPINDLE can be brought up close to workpiece for comparison to make repeat turning easy.

A HOMEMADE steady-rest is used to cut down vibrations that occur when you turn long, slender spindles.

behind the lathe to permit it to serve as a master spindle. Thus you can bring the master forward (up close) to the new workpiece for quick visual matching of the duplicate you are working on.

It is advisable to use a steady-rest to eliminate vibrations when turning the slender base spindle. If you don't have such a lathe accessory, you can easily fashion one out of wood. Simply cut a right-angle notch in a piece of wood and clamp it to the lathe bed. The corner of the angle is then set at the height of the lathe center.

It's a good idea to turn the ends of all legs and spindles just a shade under the drill size for their respective holes to allow a slight amount of play, or wobble, which is necessary to assemble the parts. When satisfied with each turning, sand it to completion before cutting off the waste.

However, don't cut off the bottom waste of the legs until the spindle holes are bored. Each of the legs requires one spindle hole bored at an angle (see drawing). This can be done simply by

propping up a flat board on the drill-press table—set at the required angle—and clamping it solidly.

For clean, positive results use spur drill bits for all boring. They should be available at your local hardware store.

Final assembly is not difficult, but do make a nonglue dry run to permit any adjustments necessary, such as shaving off a bit here and there on tight-fitting spindles.

While you're doing this, don't forget to whittle a couple of flats on all leg and spindle ends so the excess glue can escape. If you don't allow for such glue ooze-out, you'll soon discover that some of the pieces just won't bottom, but they will spring out as soon as you release them.

Plastic resin glue is a good type to use. Make a mixture that's a bit on the heavy side so it won't become too watery and runny.

Insert the armrest spindles into the sides and then add the rests. The two dowels projecting

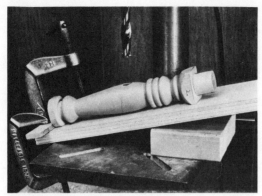

A SIMPLE DRILL-PRESS jig is necessary for boring holes in the legs. Flat ends make this trick possible.

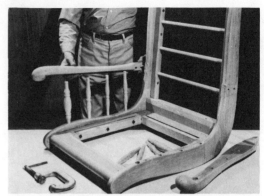

INSTALLING THE ARMREST requires a little give and take. Thus, it is best to use thick—not runny—glue.

IF SPINDLE ENDS and leg tenons are a bit smaller than the holes, the angled assembly will fit effortlessly.

WEBBING, with the ends doubled over, is nailed into the rabbeted recess. Use large-head carpet tacks.

from the rear of the arms should be sanded to a slight taper to permit some flexing of the arm so it can be worked into place over the spindles. After assembly, wipe off all excess glue; stains and finish can't penetrate a skin of glue (which actually becomes a sealer coat).

Next comes the base. Insert the spindles into the four legs. While the assembly is right-side up, apply glue to the tenons and the shoulders and also to the holes in the frame.

If possible, have a helper give you a hand to turn the assembly upside down and insert the front legs first. Then, while he holds the front legs in the right position, with a bit of twisting you can work the rear legs in place. Use one bar clamp on each leg. Since there is no place for them to go, the spindles will take care of themselves.

The finish used on the chair consists of a few coats of sanding sealer lightly sanded with 6/0 paper. Next, to a matte finish lacquer, add a bit of analine stain (cordovan may be used). Spray on a number of coats—at least three or four.

Be mindful that the stain color builds up with each pass, so don't get overzealous when you add the stain. To be sure of getting exactly the shade you want, test it on a scrap of the lumber used for the chair.

After the finish has been applied you can install the seat webbing. Using large-head upholstery tacks, double up on the ends and pull them taut. Weave each strand over and under.

To equip the chair you'll need foam cushions of the following dimensions: Seat, 4½x22x23 in.; back, 4x21x22 in.

Colonial comb box

■ A DECORATOR-INSPIRED piece for homes furnished in early American, this handsome comb box is ideal for a colonial kitchen, hall, bedroom or foyer.

Maple, pine, cherry or birch can be used to make the box and the frame for the mirror. The unit shown, however, is made of golden sumac, which, with its unusual grain, makes it appear centuries old.

The drawing below contains all the information necessary to complete the box. Just be certain to cut both of the scalloped sides identically by using a suitable pattern or template of hardboard or heavy paper to transfer the outline to the wood.

You can use glue, brads and glue, or dowels and glue to join the parts. The latter appears most authentic.

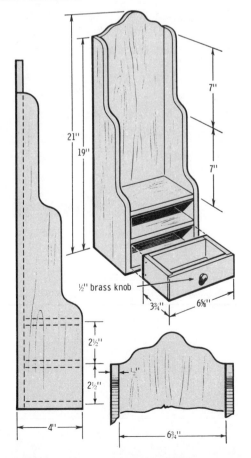

½" brass knob

21"
19"
7"
7"
2½"
2½"
3¾"
6⅝"
4"
6¾"
½"

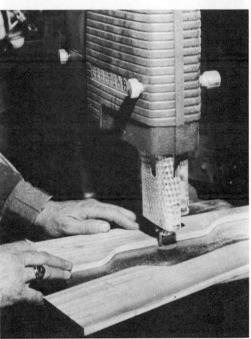

TRANSFER THE CUTTING outline to the wood stock, then cut out both sides on either a bandsaw or a jigsaw.

Modular furniture that's easy to build

■ YOU CAN CREATE a versatile module that can be used in almost any room for any purpose and lighted to suit the particular function the piece is designed for. These are good-looking furniture pieces including a handsome room divider.

The basic form with its standardized dimensions can be quickly adapted to serve any number of family needs. The idea is to get the most use from a minimal amount of space—essentially a simple enclosure measuring a foot in depth, 39½ inches in width and 84 inches in height.

The material to use on this project is ¾-in. A-D plywood. And stick to the very basic construction techniques. Simply use butt joints, glue and screws. Finishing the various pieces is a matter of personal preference. They can be painted, stained if a cabinet-grade plywood is used, or covered with plastic laminate. Or the units can be finished using a combination of two or more finishes.

ROOM DIVIDER is simplest of five handsome furniture pieces. It's accented by reflector lamps at the top.

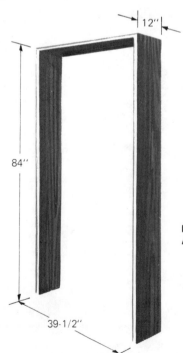

BASIC FRAMEWORK FOR ALL CONCEPTS

A modern hutch

The room divider can be used as a break-front by simply parking it along a wall. Because the shelves are of glass and the unit has three 50-watt reflector lamps, it can serve handsomely to highlight decorative objects or favored family collections. The storage space below is a bonus sure to be welcomed in most households. The beauty of the modular concept of construction is that the pieces all have the look of custom built-ins, yet should you ever move you can take the furniture with you. Wires from the lights exit through small holes in the top and are held fast to the back of the piece with insulated staples.

For a neat job, simply measure the exact length of the extension cord you will need and cut it to suit. Then attach the extension cord to the baseboard, running it along the wall using insulated staples.

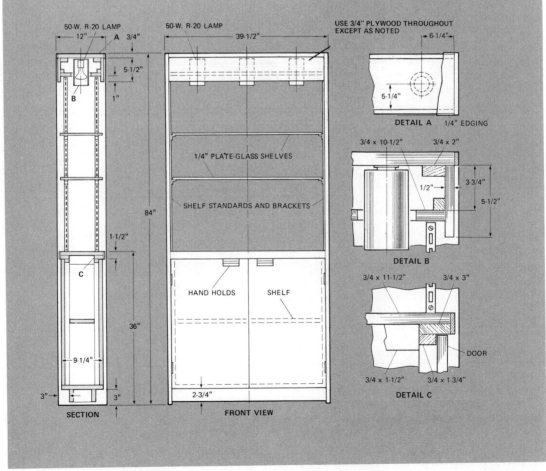

BY OPENING the lower cabinet doors to expose filing space and lowering the upper door, you get a 24-in. desktop. The lighting unit pulls out to light up the shelves and desk surface.

Versatile work or hobby bench

At first glance (see photo on next page) the closed desk appears to be a shelf-storage area. However, when you open the lower pair of doors a counter flips down and becomes a 2-ft.-deep convenient desktop. The lighting element pulls out so light is distributed both down on the desk work area and up toward the shelves where refer-ence books and knicknacks can be stored. Note the convenient file storage bins that appear on the sides of the lower doors.

For work surfaces such as the desktop, a plastic laminate should be used for durability, a smooth working surface and to keep maintenance to a minimum.

WOULD YOU believe it's a desk? When closed (right photo), unit seems to be something it's not — a breakfront. The simple structure provides necessary room for the family record-keeping.

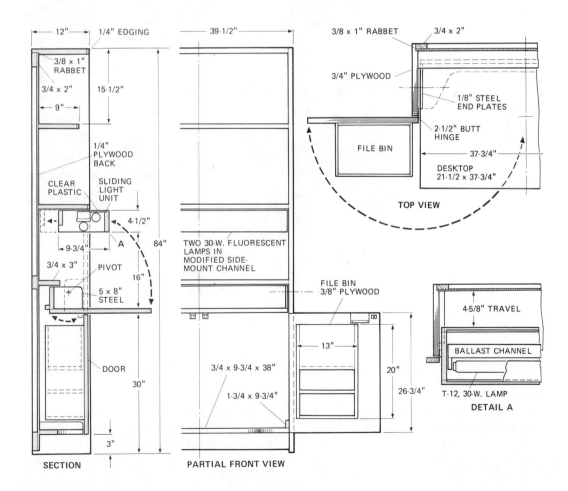

12"

1/4" EDGING

3/8 x 1" RABBET

3/4 x 2"

15-1/2"

9"

1/4" PLYWOOD BACK

CLEAR PLASTIC

SLIDING LIGHT UNIT

4-1/2"

A

9-3/4"

84"

3/4 x 3"

PIVOT

5 x 8" STEEL

16"

DOOR

30"

3"

SECTION

39-1/2"

TWO 30-W. FLUORESCENT LAMPS IN MODIFIED SIDE-MOUNT CHANNEL

FILE BIN 3/8" PLYWOOD

13"

3/4 x 9-3/4 x 38"

1-3/4 x 9-3/4

20"

26-3/4"

PARTIAL FRONT VIEW

3/8 x 1" RABBET

3/4 x 2"

3/4" PLYWOOD

1/8" STEEL END PLATES

2-1/2" BUTT HINGE

FILE BIN

37-3/4"

DESKTOP 21-1/2 x 37-3/4"

TOP VIEW

4-5/8" TRAVEL

BALLAST CHANNEL

T-12, 30-W. LAMP

DETAIL A

PERSONAL GROOMING center for the lady of the house is a scant 1 ft. deep and 39 in. wide. Height can be varied to suit the room's decor.

Vanity center

The vanity center is planned for personal grooming and can be used either sitting down or standing. Since the top surface (shelf) will not be exposed to rough treatment which might scratch or mar it, it is of ¼-in.-thick clear sheet acrylic plastic so it is possible to utilize the full-length mirror. The lighting is globe-shaped incandescent bulbs (14 25-watt No. G 18½ lamps) on both sides of the mirror and two 30-watt deluxe fluorescents in the hood overhead.

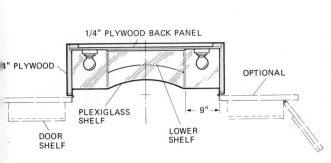

1/4" PLYWOOD BACK PANEL

4" PLYWOOD

OPTIONAL

PLEXIGLASS SHELF

9"

LOWER SHELF

DOOR SHELF

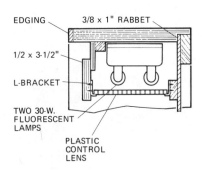

EDGING

3/8 x 1" RABBET

1/2 x 3-1/2"

L-BRACKET

TWO 30-W. FLUORESCENT LAMPS

PLASTIC CONTROL LENS

TOP VIEW

LIGHT WHERE you need it—at a makeup table: Two warm white fluorescents overhead and 14 incandescent bulbs give all you could ask for.

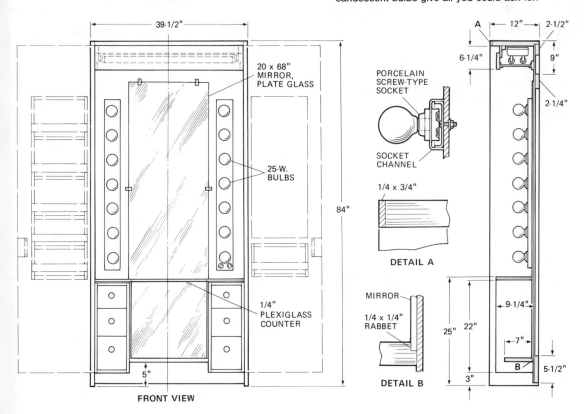

39-1/2"

20 x 68" MIRROR, PLATE GLASS

25-W. BULBS

84"

1/4" PLEXIGLASS COUNTER

5"

FRONT VIEW

A   12"   2-1/2"

PORCELAIN SCREW-TYPE SOCKET

6-1/4"   9"

2-1/4"

SOCKET CHANNEL

1/4 x 3/4"

DETAIL A

MIRROR

1/4 x 1/4" RABBET

DETAIL B

9-1/4"

25"   22"

7"

B   5-1/2"

3"

WHEN USED AS a bar-counter, the modular unit provides convenient storage under fluorescent lights.

Service bar

The same module with slight variations becomes a handy service bar with ample room for storing potables and ice cubes.

Wall systems such as these units are popular in the furniture market now, and by starting with these concepts, recognizing that sizes and designs are not fixed, you can design your own wall system at a fraction of what the commercial equivalents cost. For example, consider combining several modular elements. Two wall dividers used with a desk unit and the bar above will give about 13 ft. of wall with plenty of space. Turn your imagination loose, rearrange the wall however you want and find the arrangement that's most convenient for your current activities. You may even want to consider an L-shaped island or peninsula.

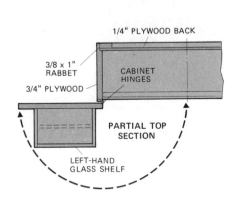

1/4" PLYWOOD BACK

3/8 x 1" RABBET

3/4" PLYWOOD

CABINET HINGES

PARTIAL TOP SECTION

LEFT-HAND GLASS SHELF

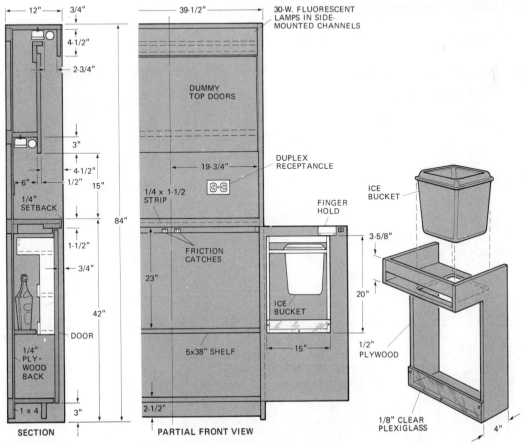

12"

3/4"

4-1/2"

2-3/4"

3"

4-1/2"

6"

1/2"

15"

1/4" SETBACK

84"

1-1/2"

3/4"

42"

DOOR

1/4" PLY-WOOD BACK

1 x 4

3"

SECTION

39-1/2"

30-W. FLUORESCENT LAMPS IN SIDE-MOUNTED CHANNELS

DUMMY TOP DOORS

DUPLEX RECEPTANCLE

19-3/4"

1/4 x 1-1/2 STRIP

FRICTION CATCHES

23"

5x38" SHELF

2-1/2"

PARTIAL FRONT VIEW

FINGER HOLD

ICE BUCKET

ICE BUCKET

15"

ICE BUCKET

3-5/8"

20"

1/2" PLYWOOD

1/8" CLEAR PLEXIGLASS

4"

Skammel stool

■ THIS NORWEGIAN milk stool, known as a skammel, is decorated with colorful rosemaling: a traditional style of painting flowers, scrolls and leaf shapes. First cut all parts, then sand them with 120-grit abrasive paper, dust and wipe with a tack cloth. Rout the decorative edge on sides (C). Cut finger slot in top (A).

Cut blind dadoes at an 80° angle in the top to create the mortises for the legs. Bevel cut one edge of each cleat (D) at 80°. Square the round dado ends with a chisel.

Glue legs in their grooves. Bore holes in cleats and attach with glue and screws to the top and legs. Glue aprons (C) in place; clamp until dry. Apply a prime coat of paint or pigmented shellac. Sand with 150-grit paper, dust and tack off. Favored colors for rosemaling are blues, greens, rusts and off-white—blended with a touch of ochre or umber from a tube of artist's pigment.

OUTSIDE THE decorative rosemaling, distinguishing feature of a skammel is fingerhole slot, by which the stool can be easily carried.

Apply two coats of background paint: rust with brown added. Use 220-grit paper between coats. Enlarge the rosemaling pattern full size and transfer it by rubbing the back with chalk or soft pencil, placing this chalked side on the wood and retracing the pattern. You can paint over chalklines. Use acrylic paints thinned to flow without dripping. Apply paints with fine-pointed artist's brushes.

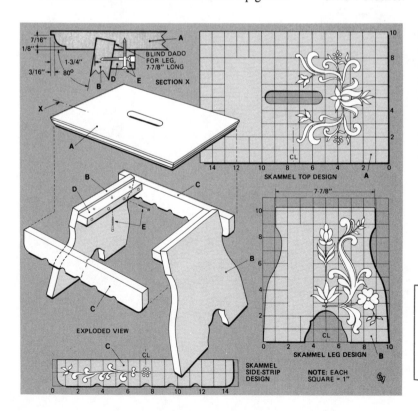

SECTION X

BLIND DADO FOR LEG, 7-7/8" LONG

7/16"
1/8"
3/16"
1-3/4"
80°

SKAMMEL TOP DESIGN

EXPLODED VIEW

SKAMMEL SIDE-STRIP DESIGN

7-7/8"

SKAMMEL LEG DESIGN

NOTE: EACH SQUARE = 1"

GLUE LEGS into blind dadoes cut at 80° angle for outward slant. Reinforce legs with beveled cleats (D).

MATERIALS LIST—SKAMMEL

Key	No.	Size and description (use)
A	1	3/4×10×15" pine (top)
B	2	3/4×10×10¼"pine (leg)
C	2	3/4×2×14¼" pine (apron)
D	2	3/4×1×7⅞" pine (cleat)
E	14	No. 7×1¼" fh brass wood screws

Misc.: Glue, primer or pigmented shellac; acrylic paints; artist's brushes.

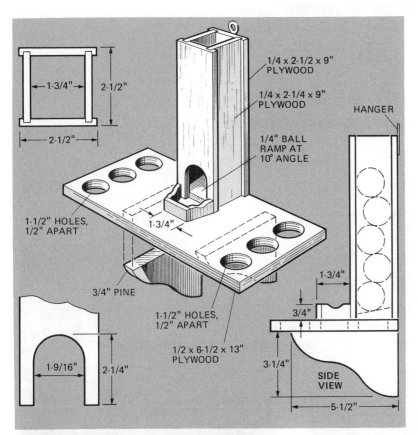

1/4 x 2-1/2 x 9" PLYWOOD

1/4 x 2-1/4 x 9" PLYWOOD

1/4" BALL RAMP AT 10° ANGLE

HANGER

1-3/4"

2-1/2"

2-1/2"

1-1/2" HOLES, 1/2" APART

1-3/4"

3/4" PINE

1-1/2" HOLES, 1/2" APART

1/2 x 6-1/2 x 13" PLYWOOD

1-9/16"

2-1/4"

1-3/4"

3/4"

3-1/4"

5-1/2"

SIDE VIEW

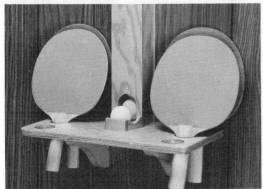

Ball and paddle caddy

■ THIS NEAT wall rack holds six table tennis paddles and stores seven balls. The balls are stored in a chimney-like dispenser that lets them roll out one at a time from an opening at the bottom.

You can make the rack of plywood leftovers from your scrap box or, for a fancier appearance, from walnut. The holes for the paddles are bored with a 1½-in. spade bit, and you'll do the neatest job if you clamp a scrap board to the underside of the plywood. A slanting block in the bottom of the ball holder makes the balls roll forward.

SIDES OF BALL HOPPER fit in grooves cut in front and back. Run grooves first, then cut ball opening in front. Insert slanting block in bottom as you glue the parts.

Flip-flop table for backgammon and chess

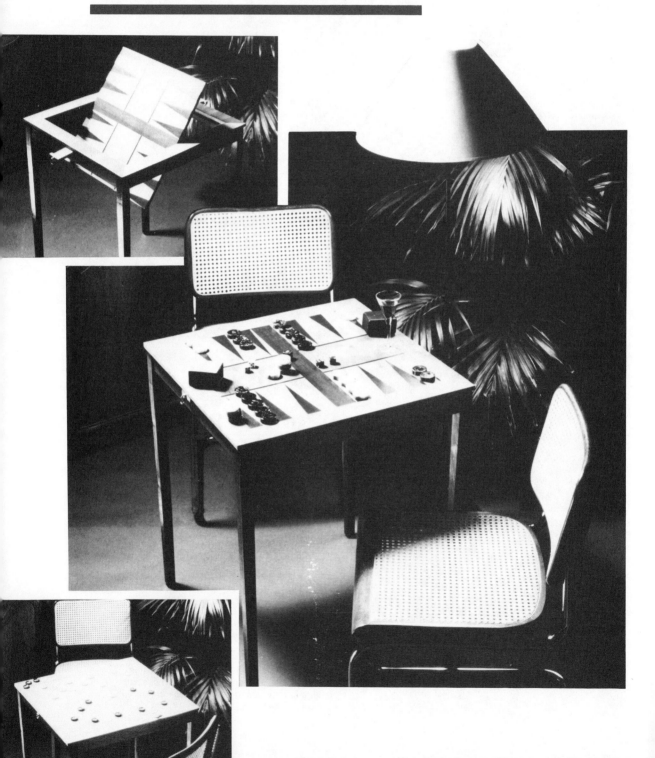

■ THIS MULTIUSE, walnut game table will look great in your den or favorite game-playing nook. The table surface is a ready-made walnut and maple veneer face with a walnut border glued to walnut plywood. The apron is also of walnut plywood (good one side), while the legs are solid walnut. All parts (except the legs and veneer faces) are cut from a ½ x 30 x 30-in. piece of walnut plywood (good one side).

Start by cutting the plywood panel for the table top with a power saw fitted with a veneer blade. Make cuts in the order numbered on cutting diagrams. Some pieces will be exact size. Others, such as the gameboard, will be oversize, to be resized later. Next, cut the gameboard panel ⅛ in. smaller than the veneer face to allow for veneer overhang at the edges.

Use veneer glue for laying the veneer faces. The backgammon and chess faces are composed of many small pieces of veneer which are held together with gum tape on the "right" side, to be peeled off later. Apply contact glue to the tape-free side, quickly and fairly heavily. Also spread glue on one side of the panel.

Allow one hour and then apply a second coat to each surface. Wait another hour before laying the veneer face on the board with a slipsheet of brown paper between to prevent premature contact. Expose ¼ in. of glued board at one edge only. When you're sure of good alignment, finger-press veneer along the exposed edge. Withdraw slipsheet gradually, about 2 in. at a time. Apply pressure with a roller, but don't roll where slipsheet is underneath. When the slipsheet has been completely removed, roll hard over entire surface in the direction of veneer grain where possible. Turn the panel over on a hard, smooth, clean surface (such as particle board) and trim off veneer overhang before gluing the second face to the panel. Sand the edge gently. Do not sand outward across the veneer face.

To remove the gum tape backing from the veneer face, moisten a 3-sq.-in. area using water and a soap-free sponge. Wait a minute for it to

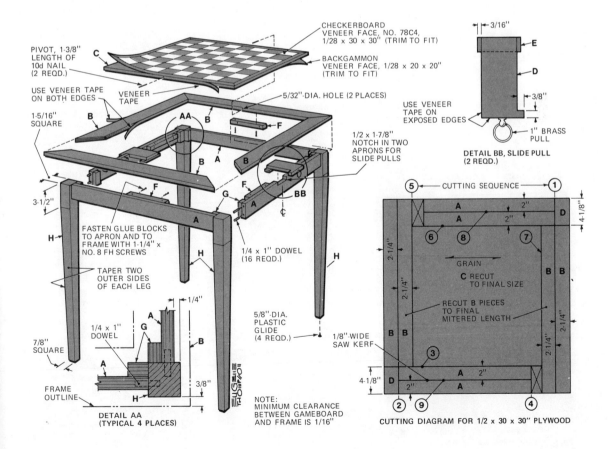

PHOTO SHOWS how to get all parts except legs from walnut plywood panel.

SPREAD GLUE on back of veneer and on plywood; recoat one hour later.

USE SLIPSHEET between coated game face and panel to assure alignment.

PRESS THE FACE with a roller for good bond and to prevent blistering.

USE A VENEER saw or X-acto knife to trim the veneer overhang.

TO REMOVE gum paper on veneer, moisten small area and scrape with chisel.

BOND VENEER trim to gameboard edges with veneer glue.

SIMPLE WOOD jig aids in boring off-center pivot holes in the frames.

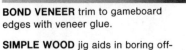

MITER FRAME members after measuring board and providing clearance.

INSERT NAIL pivots in gameboard (without glue) before assembling frame.

POSITION FRAME members around board, lay out, mark for pivot points.

ASSURE SWING clearance with 1/16-in. shims between board, frame.

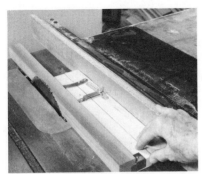

DRESS WALNUT stock for legs on jointer, taper with table saw.

NOTCH TWO aprons for slides and fasten glue blocks flush to apron tops.

PLACE SLIDES in notches. Glue and clamp board frame to understructure.

soften, then scrape with a chisel. Peel off anything that shreds. Continue this way, *resisting the temptation to soak the surface, until the board is clean.* Don't try to sand off the tape and don't use solvents.

Cover the edges of the gameboard with 1-in.-wide veneer that comes in a roll. Again, use veneer glue and the slipsheet method. Trim off the overhang.

When mitering the four pieces that frame the gameboard, allow for the thickness of the veneer edging on both the gameboard edges and on the inside edges of the frame pieces—plus a minimum $1/16$-in. clearance to permit the gameboard to pivot. Apply veneer edging to edges of frame *after* mitering.

To locate the pivot holes in two frame members and matching holes in the gameboard, lay the board on a flat surface and dry assemble four frame members around it. Measure the center point and mark it on the gameboard and frame. Drill $5/32$-in.-dia. holes at center of edges at marked locations in two opposite edges of the gameboard.

Because the gameboard, veneered on both sides, is now thicker than the $1/2$-in. frame, you have to lower the pivot hole in the frame so the gameboard top is flush with the top surface of the frame. Simply halve the thickness of the gameboard and use that dimension to locate the frame pivot hole by measuring offset from the good face. After drilling a hole in one frame member, use it as a guide for marking the second hole. A 16d nail, inserted in the hole, can be used to make a starter hole in the opposite frame member before drilling. Or use a jig to assure hole alignment.

Cut two segments of 10d nails for pivots. Working on a flat surface, insert pivots loose (no glue) in gameboard. Spread carpenter's glue on mitered ends of the frame. Lay members with walnut sides down so the frame and gameboard

are flush on the side that becomes the table top. Apply a framing clamp around the frame and use one C clamp at each corner to hold wood scrap across miters, thereby keeping the joints flat. Before tightening the framing clamps, insert eight wood or plastic scraps $1/16$ in. thick around the gameboard to obtain uniform clearance all around. After the glue is dry, remove clamps and add veneer edging around the outside edges of the frame.

For the legs, run walnut over a jointer or dress with a hand plane and then cut to length. Use a tapering jig on a table saw to taper two inside faces of each leg.

Make slides as shown. Apply veneer trim to edges and install brass ring pulls. Cut notches in two aprons for slides.

Cut glue-blocks from scrap wood and fasten to aprons with glue and screws. Then drill matching dowel holes in aprons and legs and assemble the understructure with glue.

Insert slides in their notches and glue understructure to frame/gameboard assembly. Add small glue blocks in corners to reinforce legs to aprons.

The choice of finish—varnish or oil—is yours. The gameboard should be finished before assembly. Drive furniture glides in leg bottoms.

MATERIALS LIST—GAME TABLE		
Key	Pcs.	Size and description (use)
A	4	$1/2 \times 2 \times 21\frac{1}{4}''$ walnut plywood (apron)
B	4	$1/2 \times 2\frac{1}{4} \times 24\frac{3}{4}''$ walnut plywood (frame)
C	1	$1/2 \times 19\frac{7}{8} \times 19\frac{7}{8}''$ walnut plywood (gameboard)
D	2	$1/2 \times 2\frac{1}{4} \times 4\frac{1}{8}''$ walnut plywood (slide)
E	2	$1/4 \times 3/4 \times 2\frac{1}{4}''$ walnut plywood (stop block)
F	6	$3/4 \times 3/4 \times 6''$ pine (glue blocks)
G	8	$1/2 \times 3/4 \times 2''$ walnut plywood (glue blocks)
H	4	$1\frac{5}{16} \times 1\frac{5}{16} \times 27''$ walnut (legs)

Misc.—30 × 30″ checkerboard face, 20 × 20″ backgammon veneer face, $1/4''$ doweling, 2 1″-dia. brass ring pulls, $4\frac{5}{8}''$-dia. furniture glides, $1\frac{1}{4}''$ No. 8 fh screws, veneer glue, carpenter's glue.

Shuffleboard table

■ HERE'S A GIFT the whole family can enjoy —a table shuffleboard. The waxed bed is of solid-core birch plywood with the scoring zones inlaid with strips of ⅛ x ⅛-in. walnut. The grooves for the inlays are saw kerfs made on the bench saw.

The 1x3 birch rails have interlocking joints at the corners. To make such joints, you first groove the end rails to the depth shown. Then you cut the ⅛-in. slot and tab with one cut at right angles to the groove. To make the side rails, after cutting a ⅛-in. notch in the end of the rail as shown, you turn the rail over and make a second cut to create a ⅛-in. tab. Finally, a ⅛-in. slot is made to the depth shown. To make the rubber bumpers, insert ⅛-in. dowels in surgical tubing and cement to the side rails.

The 12 weighted pucks are mass-produced from ⅝-in.-thick wood in the following manner. First the wood is clamped to the drill-press table and a ¾-in. hole is bored completely through the wood. Then, without unclamping the work, the ¾-in. bit is replaced with a hole saw and a 2-in. plug is cut completely through the wood. Next a same-size Formica disc is cut with the hole saw and cemented to the bottom of the puck. Now the outer edge of the puck is smoothed by holding it lightly against a disc sander, after which the top and bottom edges are chamfered slightly by hand with a flat file. Finally, each puck is weighted by filling the center hole with molten lead and capping with a metal chair glide. Each set of three pucks is color-coded by painting the tops.

To make the storage wells, bore 2-in. holes completely through the ¾-in. thickness. Then ⅛-in. tempered hardboard is glued to the underside and 1-in. finger holes are bored in the center of the 2-in. holes.

TABLE SHUFFLEBOARD can be a fun game for up to four people. When you make the table yourself, complete with inlaid scoring zones and weighted pucks, it adds to your enjoyment.

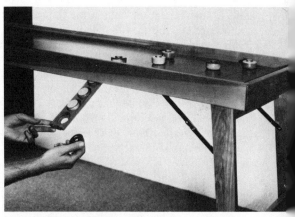

SHUFFLEBOARD weights are stored in the hinged rack beneath table. Each rack will hold six weights.

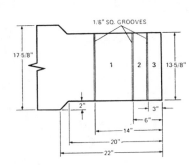

1/8" SQ. GROOVES

Rules for Shuffleboard

Number of players: Two, three or four.

Object of game is to slide weight down the table, with one rebound off side bumper, and have it land in one of three zones. Nearest zone counts one point, middle zone two points, end zone three points, overhanging weight four points. Score goes to player who has weights ahead of his opponent's. Only weights ahead of the opponent's weights are counted when you're scoring.

Each player has three weights per turn; first player to score 21 wins. Players alternate shots, scorer shoots first on next round.

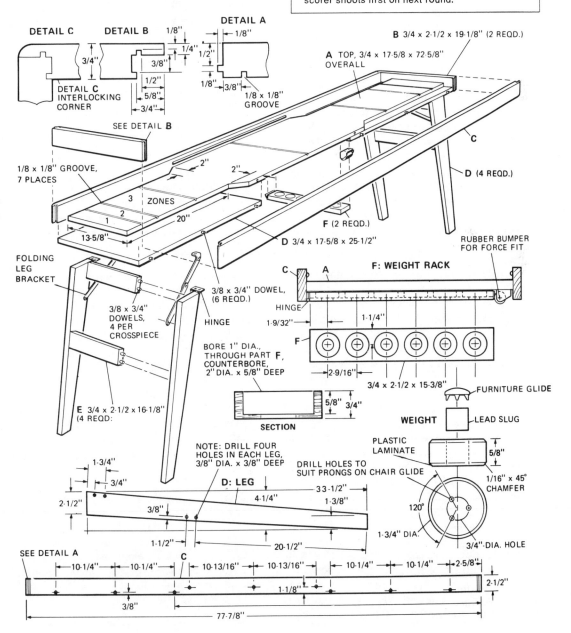

DETAIL C

DETAIL B

DETAIL A

DETAIL C INTERLOCKING CORNER

1/8 x 1/8" GROOVE

SEE DETAIL B

B 3/4 x 2-1/2 x 19-1/8" (2 REQD.)

A TOP, 3/4 x 17-5/8 x 72-5/8" OVERALL

1/8 x 1/8" GROOVE, 7 PLACES

C

D (4 REQD.)

3 ZONES

F (2 REQD.)

D 3/4 x 17-5/8 x 25-1/2"

RUBBER BUMPER FOR FORCE FIT

FOLDING LEG BRACKET

3/8 x 3/4" DOWELS, 4 PER CROSSPIECE

3/8 x 3/4" DOWEL, (6 REQD.)

HINGE

C A F: WEIGHT RACK

HINGE

1-9/32"

1-1/4"

F

2-9/16"

3/4 x 2-1/2 x 15-3/8"

FURNITURE GLIDE

BORE 1" DIA., THROUGH PART F, COUNTERBORE, 2" DIA. x 5/8" DEEP

E 3/4 x 2-1/2 x 16-1/8" (4 REQD:

SECTION

WEIGHT LEAD SLUG

NOTE: DRILL FOUR HOLES IN EACH LEG, 3/8" DIA. x 3/8" DEEP

PLASTIC LAMINATE

1/16" x 45° CHAMFER

D: LEG

DRILL HOLES TO SUIT PRONGS ON CHAIR GLIDE

120°

1-3/4" DIA.

3/4"-DIA. HOLE

SEE DETAIL A

C

Tabletop hockey game you can build

■ YOU'LL SOON FIND you have to be as quick as a fox to play hockey with an air-cushion puck. The floating puck travels at lightning speed on a cushion of air created by a fan and some 2360 tiny air jets in the playing surface.

The playing surface is made first. It consists of a ⅝-in.-thick particleboard base honeycombed with ¼-in. holes on 1-in. centers and a plastic laminate facing with an equal number of 1/16-in. holes. The particleboard is drilled first, then the laminate is cemented to it and the 1/16-in. holes drilled. The spacing and drilling of the 4720 holes is not the endless job it may seem, thanks to ¼-in. pegboard which is used as a drilling guide for both sets of holes.

Cut the particleboard, laminate and pegboard the same overall size (34⅝ x 69½ in.) and see that holes in the pegboard are centered equally along the edges. Clamp the pegboard to the top of the particleboard, edges aligned, and with a ¼-in. bit in your electric drill go from hole to hole in the pegboard.

Now cement the laminate to the particleboard with contact cement. Apply a coat to each surface, wait about 15 minutes until the cement is tacky to the touch, then bond the two together. Remember that once the coated surfaces touch, you can't shift them, so position the laminate carefully.

To drill the 1/16-in. holes using the pegboard you'll need to make a shouldered stop from a short piece of ½-in. dowel to center the bit in the ¼-in. holes. The shouldered end can be formed with the dowel chucked in your electric drill. First run a 1/16-in. bit through the center of the dowel, letting the drill protrude about ⅛ in. Then with bit and dowel still chucked in the drill, turn down the end of the dowel with a chisel so it's ¼ in. in diameter and 3/16 in. long. The tighter the dowel on the bit, the better it will resist loosening in use. Clamp the pegboard to the top of the laminate, even with the edges, and drill the 1/16-in. holes. It will take about two hours to zip through the 2360 holes.

GOALIE MALLETS AND A PUCK can be bought or made at home. Each mallet consists of three ¼-in.-thick plastic discs that are cut with a fly cutter in a drill press and cemented together. A dowel held with a screw provides a handle.

Plenum under playing surface

A bottom in the boxlike assembly forms a 2-in. air plenum under the playing surface. Make it the same size as the top and cut an opening in the center as shown to suit the blower used. You can use a range exhaust fan with two 1/25-hp, 1550-rpm motors, each driving a 3½ × 4½-in. squirrel-cage blower. The blowers put out a total of 290 C.F.M., which enters through a 4⅜ × 7¼-inch opening. You'll notice in detail A that an air baffle, slightly larger than the blower opening, is made and attached to the underside of the playing surface directly over the inlet. Make the two goal boxes to measure 3¼ × 10 in. inside and glue them to the underside of the playing surface, along with the baffle, then glue the boxes to the bottom, making sure the two panels are aligned.

Dadoes in the 6-in.-wide particleboard sides make the plenum airtight. Use glue and nails and let the ends lap the sides at the corners. It is important that the plenum be airtight. You can paint the sides or cover them with wood-grain paper. The original was faced with prefinished paneling. Here you can lap and butt the ends at the corners and hide them with outside corner molding, or just miter and glue the ends without molding. One-inch aluminum angle fitted around the top and inside provides a metal bumper for the puck. It's mitered at the corners and attached along the top with oval-head screws in countersunk holes.

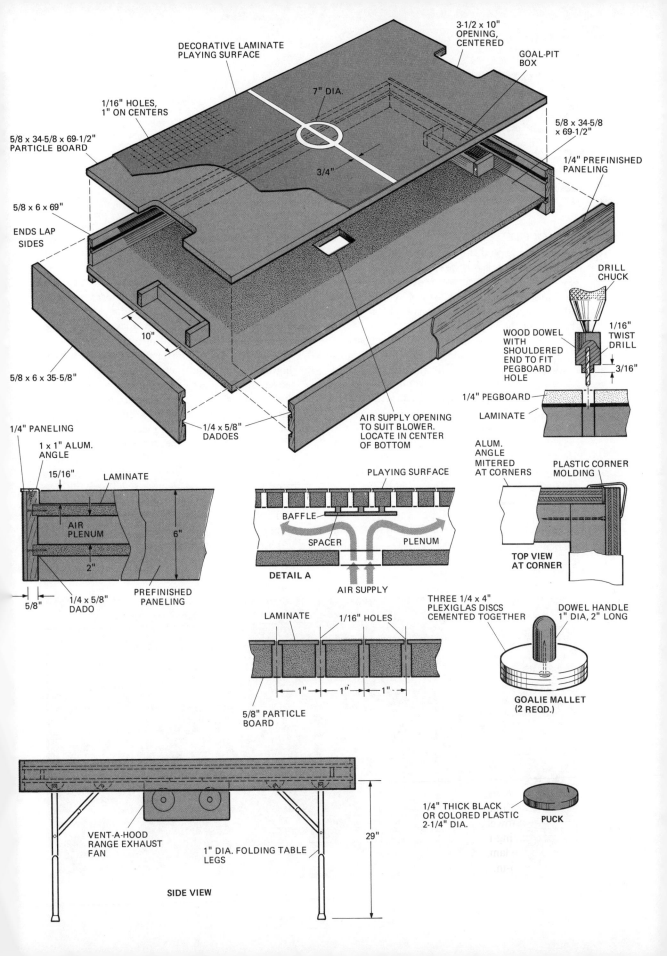

DECORATIVE LAMINATE
PLAYING SURFACE

3-1/2 x 10"
OPENING,
CENTERED

GOAL-PIT
BOX

1/16" HOLES,
1" ON CENTERS

7" DIA.

5/8 x 34-5/8
x 69-1/2"

5/8 x 34-5/8 x 69-1/2"
PARTICLE BOARD

3/4"

1/4" PREFINISHED
PANELING

5/8 x 6 x 69"

ENDS LAP
SIDES

DRILL
CHUCK

WOOD DOWEL
WITH
SHOULDERED
END TO FIT
PEGBOARD
HOLE

1/16"
TWIST
DRILL

3/16"

1/4" PEGBOARD

LAMINATE

10"

5/8 x 6 x 35-5/8"

1/4 x 5/8"
DADOES

AIR SUPPLY OPENING
TO SUIT BLOWER.
LOCATE IN CENTER
OF BOTTOM

ALUM.
ANGLE
MITERED
AT CORNERS

PLASTIC CORNER
MOLDING

1/4" PANELING

1 x 1" ALUM.
ANGLE

15/16"

LAMINATE

AIR PLENUM

6"

2"

5/8"

1/4 x 5/8"
DADO

PREFINISHED
PANELING

PLAYING SURFACE

BAFFLE

SPACER

PLENUM

DETAIL A

AIR SUPPLY

TOP VIEW
AT CORNER

THREE 1/4 x 4"
PLEXIGLAS DISCS
CEMENTED TOGETHER

DOWEL HANDLE
1" DIA, 2" LONG

LAMINATE

1/16" HOLES

1"

1"

1"

5/8" PARTICLE
BOARD

GOALIE MALLET
(2 REQD.)

VENT-A-HOOD
RANGE EXHAUST
FAN

1" DIA. FOLDING TABLE
LEGS

29"

1/4" THICK BLACK
OR COLORED PLASTIC
2-1/4" DIA.

PUCK

SIDE VIEW

Chess set fit for a king

■ THOUGH ITS EXACT origin is unknown, a generally accepted theory is that chess was imported to Europe from the Orient more than 1500 years ago. The game as we know it today, except for minor changes, is at least 600 years old. The rules, pieces, and board have not changed through all those years.

While the shapes and sizes of the chessmen may vary, the checkered playing board is standardized around the world and consists of 64 squares—32 light colored and 32 dark. Here we present an elegant modern version of the old board and pieces. In our version, the board is of ½-in. plywood and the squares are made by tilting the table saw blade to 45° and running shallow V-grooves at right angles.

The contemporary chessmen are machined on a metal lathe. One set is of brass while the other is of aluminum so the opposing men can be readily identified. Other combinations of metal could be used or both sets could be aluminum with one set being anodized. To protect them when not in use, they are snugly stored in rattleproof drawers lined with styrofoam. Pieces can be placed here when captured, or stored here when the game is not in use.

Making the chessmen: Start by cutting the stock to length—allowing two pieces to each length—except for the kings and queens. Cut a piece out on one end of the stock, then reverse the stock end for end and turn the second piece. Dimensions for all the pieces are given with a high degree of accuracy in the diagram; use standard metal-lathe practice to cut them. The stylized king's crown is made using a jeweler's file. Carefully file the notches about ¹⁄₁₆ in. wide and ¹⁄₁₆ in. deep. The other pieces can all be made using just the metal lathe. Note that the knight is not the traditional horse.

Finishing the chessmen: After each piece has been turned, leave it mounted and polish it dry with 240-grit emery cloth, then with oil. Next use 320 grit, also dry and then with oil. Use lacquer thinner and tissue paper to clean the piece while it is still on the lathe. Once each of the pieces has been cleaned make certain that they are not touched with the fingers.

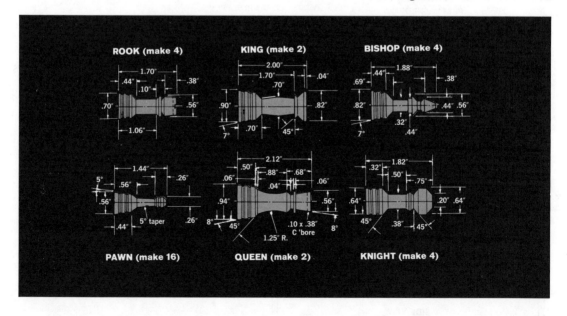

Heat the piece with a torch until just warm—don't overheat. Then apply three coats of spray-can lacquer to provide good, thorough protection for each piece. Finally, cut the piece off with a parting tool, making sure the bottom is flat. If there are any burrs, knock them off with a single-cut file or the piece may not sit flat.

The aluminum pieces were flocked (on the bottoms) with a royal blue flock and the brass pieces received a light green flock. (Flocking is the process of applying powdered felt to paint while it is still wet. Here, of course, it is applied to lacquer.) The felt on the bases is optional, but it does save the playing board from scratches, which means it will look its best much longer.

Making the cabinet: Start by cutting the playing board to size. Be sure you allow an extra ⅛ in. on all four sides for inserting the plywood into dadoes in the cabinet sides. After grooving the squares, sand the board thoroughly, and stain alternate squares, using an artist's brush and walnut stain. Each player should have a light square in the righthand corner.

Next make the box. There are no tricky or unusual cabinetmaking techniques called for, but work carefully so that the finished product will have the look of elegance it deserves. The

LATHE-TURNED MEN in gleaming brass and aluminum, used and stored in a rich walnut case, make this handsome chess set a unique conversation piece that's worthy of your finest craftsmanship. Each set is stored in a drawer of its own and is cradled in a bed of styrofoam. The chess playing surface is scored and squares are stained contrasting light and dark colors. *NOTE:* The board, as shown here, is set up incorrectly. Each player should have a *light* square in the righthand corner. Decide whether you want the drawers to open *toward* the players, or to each *side*, before staining the squares.

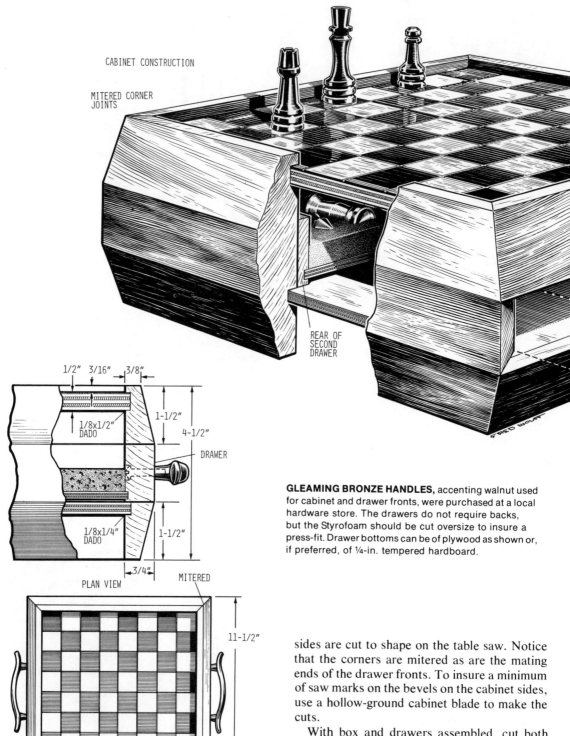

CABINET CONSTRUCTION

MITERED CORNER JOINTS

REAR OF SECOND DRAWER

1/2" 3/16" 3/8"

1-1/2"

4-1/2"

1/8x1/2" DADO

DRAWER

1-1/2"

1/8x1/4" DADO

3/4"

PLAN VIEW

MITERED

11-1/2"

11-1/2"

GLEAMING BRONZE HANDLES, accenting walnut used for cabinet and drawer fronts, were purchased at a local hardware store. The drawers do not require backs, but the Styrofoam should be cut oversize to insure a press-fit. Drawer bottoms can be of plywood as shown or, if preferred, of ¼-in. tempered hardboard.

sides are cut to shape on the table saw. Notice that the corners are mitered as are the mating ends of the drawer fronts. To insure a minimum of saw marks on the bevels on the cabinet sides, use a hollow-ground cabinet blade to make the cuts.

With box and drawers assembled, cut both styrofoam drawer liners to size. Next, arrange the chessmen in two rows as they appear on the board. Then, gently press each piece down into the Styrofoam so that it will clear the drawer

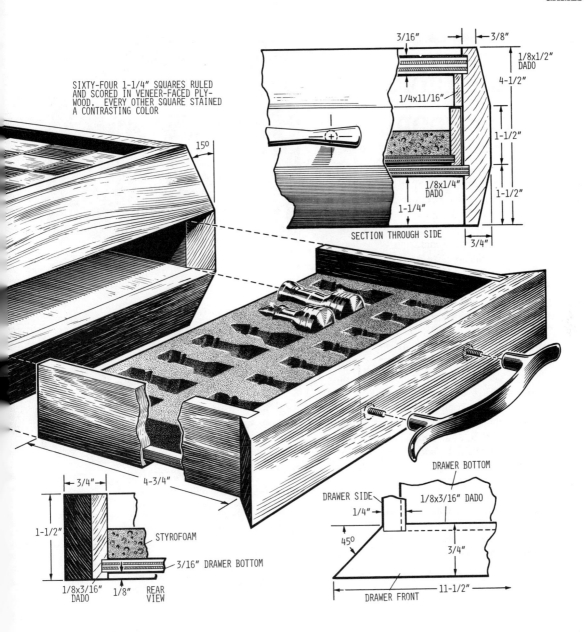

SIXTY-FOUR 1-1/4" SQUARES RULED AND SCORED IN VENEER-FACED PLYWOOD. EVERY OTHER SQUARE STAINED A CONTRASTING COLOR

15°

3/16"   3/8"

1/8x1/2" DADO

4-1/2"

1/4x11/16"

1-1/2"

1/8x1/4" DADO

1-1/2"

1-1/4"

3/4"

SECTION THROUGH SIDE

DRAWER BOTTOM

DRAWER SIDE   1/8x3/16" DADO

1/4"

45°   3/4"

11-1/2"

DRAWER FRONT

3/4"   4-3/4"

1-1/2"   STYROFOAM

3/16" DRAWER BOTTOM

1/8x3/16" DADO   1/8   REAR VIEW

opening. Remove the pieces, paint the styrofoam top and front and then flock with the color of your choice. Allow ample time for the setup to dry before going on to the next step. *Caution:* Since certain paints will melt Styrofoam, check the label carefully when selecting the paint.

Being an open-grain wood, the walnut does require filling. To do it, make a paste, mixed to about the consistency of heavy cream, using walnut filler and walnut oil stain. Rubbing with

the grain, work the filler into the open pores of the wood. To remove the excess, wipe off with strokes across the grain so that the filler remains packed in the pores. This is standard procedure any time you use paste wood filler on a fine woodworking project. Allow the cabinet to dry for at least 24 hours. To finish, apply two or three coats of lacquer. When this is dry, apply a paste wax and buff it to a soft luster.

With the board and men finished you are ready to take on your opponent in the best of style!

Game table for your playroom

■ HERE'S A WORKSHOP project that will provide hours of enjoyment for your family and friends. It's a family game table for most any game you want to play and, best of all, it's easy to construct with basic lumberyard materials.

Basically, the table consists of three circular assemblies—a bottom chip-and-glass tray, a center disc, and a felt-covered top—all cut from A-D plywood to nest one on top of the other.

You start with the center disc. If you have a router, you can cut a perfect circle by tethering it to a strip of wood with a nail in the end. If you don't have a router, use your sabre saw. Four quarter-circle segments are cut from ¼-in. plywood and nailed to the underside of the center disc to form a tray. Then the edge of the disc is "wrapped" with a 1-in.-wide strip of ¼-in. hardboard and nailed and glued. Next, eight glass-holder dividers are added equidistant around the plywood tray, four of them being placed over the butted joints.

Finally, the outer edge is wrapped with a double strip of hardboard. Glue and nail one at a time and place the joints of the two strips 180° apart. The top playing surface is a ⅜-in. plywood disc, which is covered with green felt. The legs screw into metal mounting plates you can buy.

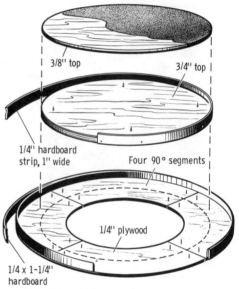

3/8" top

3/4" top

¼" hardboard strip, 1" wide

Four 90° segments

¼" plywood

1/4 x 1-1/4" hardboard

HOW THE PARTS SANDWICH TOGETHER

FELT CAN BE STRETCHED without puckering if you first staple one edge and then the edge opposite.

OPTIONAL SUPPORT

Card table can be used to support top if you wish

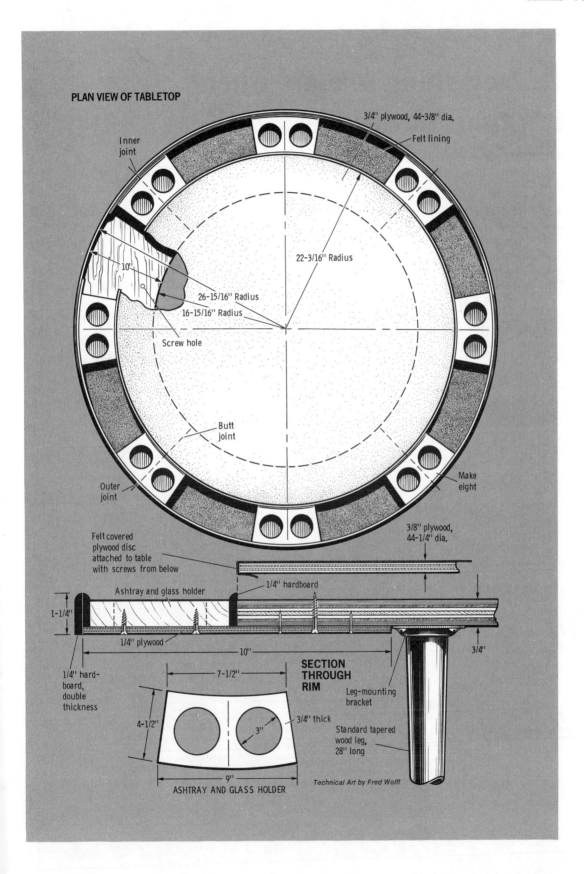

PLAN VIEW OF TABLETOP

Inner joint

3/4" plywood, 44-3/8" dia.

Felt lining

22-3/16" Radius

26-15/16" Radius

16-15/16" Radius

10"

Screw hole

Butt joint

Outer joint

Make eight

3/8" plywood, 44-1/4" dia.

Felt covered plywood disc attached to table with screws from below

Ashtray and glass holder

1/4" hardboard

1/4" hardboard

1-1/4"

1/4" plywood

10"

3/4"

SECTION THROUGH RIM

Leg-mounting bracket

1/4" hardboard, double thickness

7-1/2"

4-1/2"

3"

3/4" thick

Standard tapered wood leg, 28" long

9"

ASHTRAY AND GLASS HOLDER

Technical Art by Fred Wolf!

Everything's ready when it's time for bridge

■ IT'S TIME for bridge—do you know where your playing cards are? You will if you keep them in this attractive holder that stores two decks of cards, pencils and a score pad. If made of select hardwood and given a rich hand-rubbed finish, it makes a handsome desk or shelf accessory. It requires a lathe to turn its pedestal base and the lipped pencil well. However, if you lack a lathe, you can alter the shape of these parts and make them square for easy cutting on your table or radial saw.

Cut the top, bottom, ends and side pieces in pairs from ¼-in.-thick walnut or cherry. Jigsaw two card slots on the top and bore a 1-in. hole in the center; bore a ⅝-in. hole in the bottom; assemble the parts. Note that ¹⁄₁₆-in.-deep rabbets are cut along all four edges of top and bottom pieces. The side and end pieces fit flush in the recesses formed by these rabbets. The dividers forming the card wells must be in place before the rest of the parts are actually put together in the assembled form.

Turn the pedestal from a 3¼-in.-sq. block of solid stock and form a tenon ¼ x ⅝-in. at the top.

The pedestal can be finished while it is still spinning in the lathe. Since it would be difficult to finish the score-pad rack after it's attached to the holder, finish it before assembly. Then cover the bottom with felt held on with white glue, and you are ready to call your bridge group.

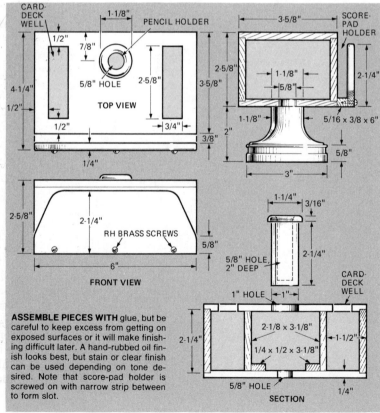

CARD-DECK WELL

1-1/8"

PENCIL HOLDER

SCORE-PAD HOLDER

1/2"

7/8"

5/8" HOLE

2-5/8"

TOP VIEW

4-1/4"

1/2"

1/2"

3-5/8"

3/4"

3/8"

1/4"

3-5/8"

2-5/8"

1-1/8"

5/8"

1-1/8"

5/16 x 3/8 x 6"

5/8"

2"

3"

2-1/4"

2-5/8"

2-1/4"

RH BRASS SCREWS

5/8"

6"

FRONT VIEW

1-1/4"

3/16"

2-1/4"

5/8" HOLE, 2" DEEP

1" HOLE

1"

CARD-DECK WELL

2-1/4"

2-1/8 x 3-1/8"

1-1/2"

1/4 x 1/2 x 3-1/8"

5/8" HOLE

1/4"

SECTION

ASSEMBLE PIECES WITH glue, but be careful to keep excess from getting on exposed surfaces or it will make finishing difficult later. A hand-rubbed oil finish looks best, but stain or clear finish can be used depending on tone desired. Note that score-pad holder is screwed on with narrow strip between to form slot.

This was once an attached garage

■ SEEKING A SPACIOUS family entertainment center close to the kitchen, one family chose to utilize the already attached garage for that "addition." The decision not only eliminated architectural design problems, but, in fact, improved the exterior appearance because the garage doors—which faced the street—were replaced with windows that are completely compatible with those in the existing house. And, as can be seen from these pictures, what the owners saved on structural costs they used for a detailed, and very elegant, interior-finish treatment.

They decided that the creation of a cathedral ceiling meant that the joists (called collar beams in a garage) would have to go. Without them, the roof would very likely sag under a heavy load, so they called in a contractor to solve the problem.

The first thing done was to snake in a 6 × 12-in. beam beneath the ridgeboard. This transferred the roof load to the ground via spiked-together 2 × 10-in. headers over the studs. The existing rafters were then tied into the new beam. [*PM's architect simplifies construction even further (as shown in the drawing) and he assures us it is equally sound structurally. Either way, after drafting your plans, you are well advised to discuss the project with your local building department. Proper weight transferral to the ground is too important to leave to guesswork. And almost every job is different because of variables such as length of ridge, rafter-run and the like.*]

Next, full-thick, foil-face insulation was installed between rafters and the ceiling was skinned with ½-in. plasterboard. Simulated rafters were added (to divide the ceiling) at 6½-ft. intervals. Finally, for acoustical reasons, the plasterboard ceiling was sprayed with textured cement-type paint.

Floor. It was necessary to remove the existing concrete floor along three sides of the outside perimeter in order to dig a trench to contain the heat ducts. To minimize heat loss, 1-in. Styro-

THE REMODELED EXTERIOR shows windows chosen to fill the old garage-door opening. Interior can be duplicated by a careful craftsman.

foam was placed along the footings. Next, the concrete was leveled to match the existing floor and 6-mil polyethylene was placed over the floor to cut down any chance of moisture damage to carpeting from below.

In this home, the original heating plant was large enough to take on the added room. In many homes this may not hold true. If you have any doubt about the B.T.U. output of your furnace, consult a heating expert. Whether you have to

THE FIREPLACE and hearth form the focal center of the room. Decorative panel-inserts flanking fireplace have dimmer-controlled lights behind.

add heating or can utilize your existing plant, the room should be controlled by its own thermostat for greatest comfort.

Fireplace. Though admittedly its size makes it a luxury, the owner decided to install an oversize fireplace. (The opening is approximately 4½ ft. wide by 3 ft. high.) Because of these dimensions, extra footings were installed to support the structure. For textural contrast with the paneled walls, the hearth was constructed of smooth-cut stone while the fireplace face was skinned with a lightweight volcanic stone. Built-ins which flank the fireplace are a matter of personal taste. If your budget is limited, they can always be added later.

Walls. Framing, as shown in the drawing, is the conventional stud-wall. In the garage-door opening, holes were bored in the slab, and after some concrete was slushed in, anchor bolts for holding the sole plate were dropped in place.

From this point on, all construction was standard with the exception of the recessed paneled walls. Like the ceiling, the walls were insulated with full-thick batts and covered with ½-in. plasterboard. To insure against drafts, joints were taped and spackled as were all countersunk nailheads.

Use prefinished paneling

Next, if you're duplicating the room, apply ¼-in. prefinished paneling over the drywall using mastic and nails. Then carefully measure the four walls for height and length to determine exact placement of the 1 x 6 vertical and horizontal framing members. Once these are up, it is simply a matter of mitering and placing the base-cap molding which surrounds each recessed panel. Bear in mind when selecting the paneling that you will have to match and stain those 1 x 6 members and moldings. How much of a job this will be depends in part on the type of paneling you choose.

The look of old-world craftsmanship that this room boasts is actually achieved mostly through the use of stock moldings. (Even the dentil is available at lumber-yards.)

Lighting. At the angle between roof and wall, a decorative alcove was installed to conceal fluorescent fixtures, controlled by a switch within the room.

The experienced do-it-yourselfer can probably handle most of the job—including the fireplace, which can be a relatively simple chore if you install one of the many factory-built versions that are self-insulating and require no footings.

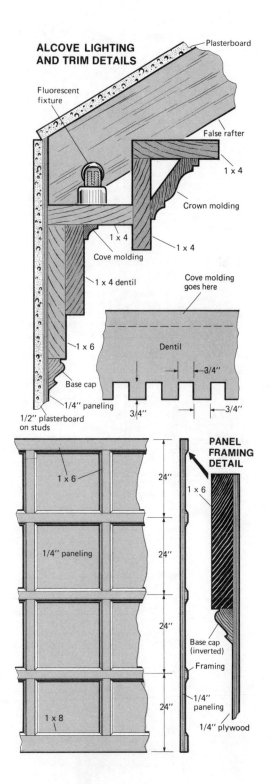

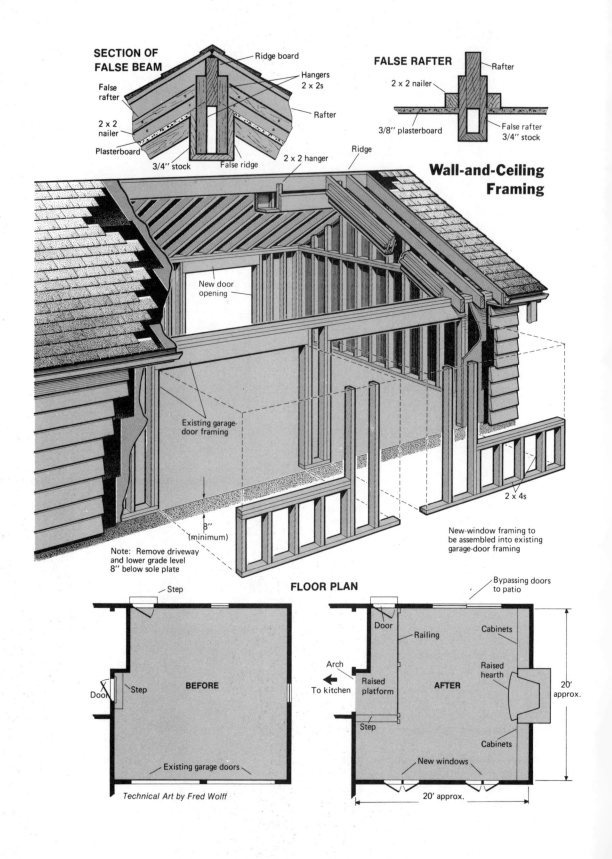

SECTION OF FALSE BEAM

Ridge board

Hangers 2 x 2s

False rafter

Rafter

2 x 2 nailer

Plasterboard

3/4'' stock

False ridge

2 x 2 hanger

Ridge

FALSE RAFTER

Rafter

2 x 2 nailer

3/8'' plasterboard

False rafter 3/4'' stock

Wall-and-Ceiling Framing

New door opening

Existing garage-door framing

8'' (minimum)

Note: Remove driveway and lower grade level 8'' below sole plate

2 x 4s

New-window framing to be assembled into existing garage-door framing

FLOOR PLAN

Step

Door

Step

BEFORE

Arch

To kitchen

Door

Existing garage doors

Technical Art by Fred Wolff

Bypassing doors to patio

Door

Railing

Cabinets

Raised hearth

Raised platform

AFTER

20' approx.

Step

Cabinets

New windows

20' approx.

This was once a detached garage

■ A LARGE PART of the fun of having a second home in the country is that you can have friends and relatives out for visits. However, extended visits often crowd the hosts as well as their guests. Weary of this inconvenience, an enterprising couple recently looked about their property to see what they could do about getting the room they often needed.

They first considered an addition to the main house. Contractor cost estimates, and the news that their year-old heating plant would have to be replaced because it could not warm additional

BEFORE: Three-car garage offered 560 sq. ft.

AFTER: Same building, a comfortable guest house.

WICKER FURNITURE comfortably seats six or seven without crowding the room.

KITCHEN-DINING AREA. All needed appliances are in the unit next to the half-wall.

BEDROOM NO. 2 has ample space for two beds, roomy dresser and a nightstand.

THE HIGH-RISER used in the bedroom is a sofa by day, converts to a pair of beds by night.

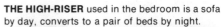

space, quickly discouraged them. Next, they looked at the usually vacant three-car garage located 150 feet from the house proper. This, they decided, would be their guest house.

Such a conversion is logical for several reasons:

1. Because the structure (shell) is already there, cost of building is sharply reduced.

2. A "guest room" set apart would assure guests and hosts complete privacy.

3. If they chose, the little house could be rented to help defray the cost.

Alterations were kept simple; no unusual or custom-built features were planned or incorporated. The biggest job on the shell was to close up the wall where the garage doors originally were located, and to install a 9-ft.-wide, sliding-door unit. The sliding-door unit selected is easy to assemble and install. Two men did this job in one day.

Perhaps the hardest part of the job was selecting the material to use for the interior. The small rooms demanded crisp, clean decorating which would create an illusion of spaciousness. At the same time, the man of the house wanted an inte-

Fitting paneling around the windows is done by holding the panel in place and marking directly from window

PANELING is secured in place by driving precolored nails that match the panel color.

WINDOW CUTOUT in panel is made from the back side, using a circular saw. To start, use a vertical plunge.

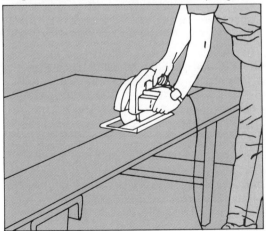

SOUTH WALL OF GARAGE prior to conversion. Peachtree aluminum sliding doors were installed.

LAST STEP is to install the door itself. Door shown is fully weatherstripped.

WALL SECTION comes down fast. Because wall was first framed, there is no need for temporary support.

TRIPLE-WINDOW MULLION was installed in the wall which replaced garage doors on the original front.

TWO MEN PUSH FRAME into the opening. After plumbing frame with level, it is fastened to studs.

rior that would require minimum maintenance. Both problems were solved by covering all walls and ceilings with a slightly off-white paneling with a textured look. Its finish is tough, and care consists of nothing more than an occasional wiping.

While limited space did not permit a bathtub, the $5\frac{1}{2} \times 7$-ft. bathroom does have a full-size shower. Also, because of its size, the house had to be carefully decorated. Old wicker furniture was resurrected, scrubbed down and painted white, and fabrics were then selected to complete the light, spacious feeling of the rooms. The attractive bedroom furniture groupings and the shutters were selected from a mail order catalog.

Floors in the family room and bedrooms were covered with shag carpeting over a polyethylene vapor barrier, while kitchen and bath were treated with seamless vinyl covering.

Garage space-saver

■ HAS YOUR GARAGE gradually turned into just a storage barn? Well, here's an easy way to add enough storage space so you can clear an area to park the car. This project requires only minimal carpentry experience, no special tools, and all materials are stock items.

Plan for materials

Count the studs along the wall where your platform will be located. For every two studs you'll need one length of 2 x 6 for the floor joist, one 2 x 4 upright to connect the joist to the rafter, two ½-in. plywood gusset plates (figure about 3½ x 10 in. for each) to attach the upright to the rafter, and ⁵⁄₁₆ x 4-in. bolts with washers.

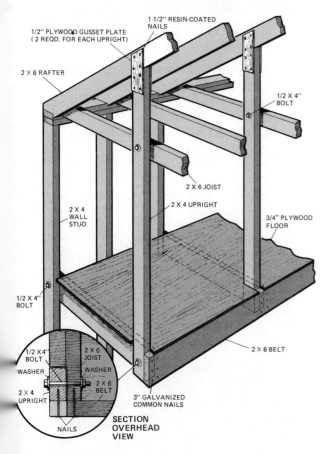

1/2" PLYWOOD GUSSET PLATE
(2 REQD. FOR EACH UPRIGHT)

1-1/2'' RESIN-COATED NAILS

2 X 6 RAFTER

1/2 X 4''
BOLT

2 X 6 JOIST

2 X 4 UPRIGHT

2 X 4
WALL
STUD

3/4" PLYWOOD
FLOOR

1/2 X 4''
BOLT

2 X 6 BELT

1/2 X 4''
BOLT

WASHER

2 X 4
UPRIGHT

2 X 6
JOIST

WASHER

2 X 6
BELT

3'' GALVANIZED
COMMON NAILS

NAILS

SECTION
OVERHEAD
VIEW

PUT AN END to clutter in your garage with this strong storage platform. You can build it level with the top of the wall or a few feet down for extra storage. Either is a low-cost way to add ''floor space.''

Once you've picked the location, mark a level line across the wall studs where the 2 x 6s connect. Then measure 4 ft. along each sidewall to allow for the plywood platform. Using a level, carry this mark up the wall until you reach the rafter. **Tip:** If you make careful measurements along the outside walls, you can mark all the rafters and studs accurately by snapping a chalkline held between your measured marks.

Here's how to figure the right lengths for the joists and uprights. For the joists you have to allow 3½ in. for bolting to the wall stud, plus 4 ft. under the plywood platform, less 1½ in. under the platform for the run of the 2 x 6 belt. Total length: 50 in. The length of the uprights will depend on where you mount the platform. Measure from your mark on the rafter to the bottom of the 2 x 6 joist and remember to allow for the angle cut where the upright and the rafter meet. The only other piece of framing you'll need is a single length of 2 x 6 for the belt. It stiffens the assembly and supports the outside edge of the plywood between the joists.

Building the platform

After cutting your materials to the proper lengths, attach the joists to the wall studs. **Tip:** Tack the joist in position and clamp it. Then drill through both pieces (the hole alignment is automatically correct) and install the bolt. This procedure can be used at every bolted joint.

Make the angle cut on your uprights and then nail the gusset plates to them. Spot a few nails on the free ends of the plates. This way, as you raise the upright to your mark, the plates sandwich the rafter and you can lock the joint easily. A coat of a preservative will help keep the platform in good shape.

VERSATILE AND practically indestructible, hanging wall bins are capable of doing a job that shelves just cannot match. They resist oil, gasoline and a variety of mild acids.

Increase your garage storage space

■ NEXT TO MONEY and cheap gasoline, the commodity most people never seem to have enough of is storage space. Even if you're not a pack rat and try to keep your inventory of accumulated material to a minimum, you almost always end up looking for more places to put things.

You can build a loft out of just about anything, but we decided to use slotted angle iron rather than wood for the main support beams. The virtue of using slotted angle iron is that you can assemble it with nuts and bolts and easily disassemble it if you need to modify the design or expand on it later. Wood just doesn't give you that ease of flexibility.

A STORAGE LOFT is an ideal way to store items that you need to use only occasionally.

THE METAL BRACKET for the storage bins can be installed right to the wall with screws or lagbolts.

STEEL CHEST of drawers will literally hold a ton of fasteners and other small parts and wire.

ONCE BRACKET is installed, bins attach by press-fitting lips at back of bins into channels.

The first thing you have to decide is how high the loft should be. That may sound like an obvious bit of logic, but keep in mind that it not only has to be high enough to allow you to work underneath, but must also be high enough to clear your car's raised hood with the front end of the car jacked up. Overhead clearance is especially important if you own a pickup truck.

Once you've established the height, you can assemble the four uprights. We attached "feet" to the uprights and anchored the feet into the cement floor. Ideally, you should tuck the loft into a corner of the garage. That way, you will be able to anchor three of the uprights to the walls and ensure adequate vertical rigidity.

Since we planned to use sheets of 4x8 plywood for the platform, we placed the uprights 8 ft. apart. Once the three uprights were anchored to the walls, the free-standing upright was anchored to the floor and the lateral platform pieces were bolted in.

After the perimeter of the platform was installed, we bolted in two stiffening ribs in the middle of the platform to support the plywood sheets.

In using angle iron, we've discovered that nuts tend to get loose and back off the bolts. We cured that problem by using Loctite on the bolts before screwing on the nuts and torquing them down. You can paint the underside of the loft white and install a light fixture. It gave us quite a large light-reflecting surface and kept the loft from looking like a cave.

One of the neatest ways we found of storing odd, but frequently needed, bits and pieces, was to use hanging storage bins. These heavy plastic bins can be stacked on top of each other if you want them to be mobile, or they can be hung on a wall with a metal bracket.

The bins attach to the bracket by press-fitting the lips at the back of the bins into the slots on the bracket. No other fasteners are used, which makes the whole setup very versatile if you need to use the bins elsewhere.

The last piece of storage equipment we've found invaluable for holding nuts, bolts, solderless connectors, wire, clamps, and the like is a steel chest of drawers. This piece will hold just about everything you'll ever need. If you outgrow it, you'll probably be ready to open your own hardware store.

Garage door maintenance

■ SOME PEOPLE NEVER have trouble with their garage doors. Others start having headaches the day the doors are installed.

Why? There are actually eight reasons.

1. Enough forces are working against a door to knock it out of adjustment.

2. Bolts, screws and lags holding hardware can loosen in time.

3. Wooden doors often absorb moisture and get too heavy for simple spring adjustment.

4. Rainy spells will also cause wooden doors and stops to swell, creating binding and friction.

5. Anything added to the door after initial adjustment and balance (such as glass, decorations, even paint) increases weight and can throw the springs out of balance.

6. Dirt in the tracks increases friction.

7. Lack of lubrication or dirty lubricant will also add to door problems.

8. Any physical damage to either the doors or tracks will affect their operation.

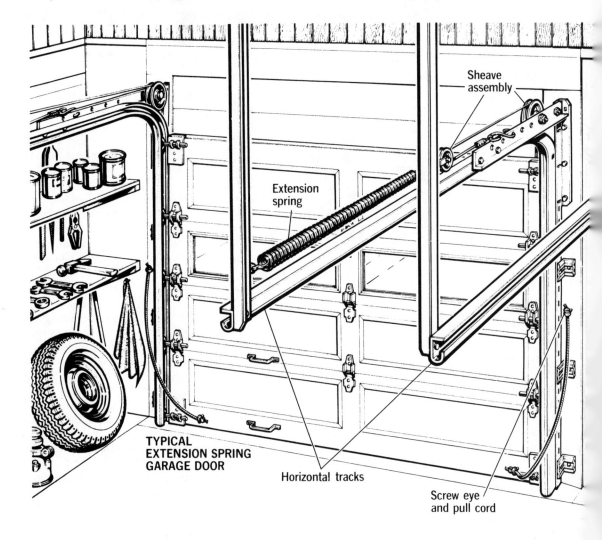

Sheave assembly

Extension spring

TYPICAL EXTENSION SPRING GARAGE DOOR

Horizontal tracks

Screw eye and pull cord

These eight factors will affect both extension-spring and torsion-spring overhead-type doors. The extension-spring type, identified by springs along both horizontal tracks, is the easiest to work on—you can repair and adjust it yourself.

The torsion-spring door is identified by torsion springs wrapped around a shaft that can be seen across the top of the door when it is closed. Cables in a torsion-spring setup wind on winch-like drums attached to the same shaft as the springs.

Here's the only rub—you shouldn't attempt to adjust torsion springs by yourself. According to one door manufacturer, "The only way spring force of a torsion-spring door can be increased is by winding the springs additional turns. This requires two bars to hold the winding plugs. The springs are under tremendous tension and someone who has had no experience in the job can be seriously injured. We recommend a professional if adjustment is required to any torsion-spring setup, other than oiling and adjusting of hardware."

Get a diagram calling out the specific parts of your particular door. The manufacturer of the door will usually supply it if you give the right information. Look for a name and serial number plate near the lock. Tell the manufacturer the width and height of the door, its material (wood, fiberglass, steel), model name (if available), serial number and approximate age.

Now let's take each major door problem and see how to handle it.

Friction, for instance, is the most prevalent.

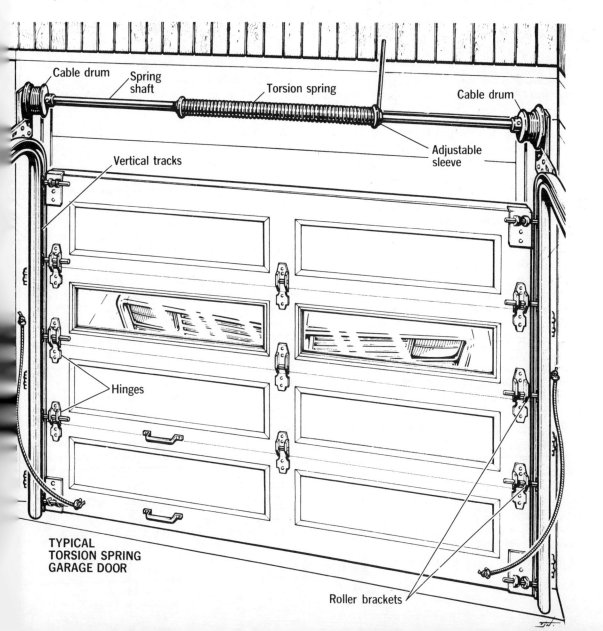

Cable drum Spring shaft Torsion spring Cable drum Adjustable sleeve Vertical tracks Hinges Roller brackets

TYPICAL TORSION SPRING GARAGE DOOR

REDUCING FRICTION between the door and the track (left) or the door and the stop (right) requires bolt adjustment.

To cure it, use a fairly heavy grade of oil (No. 20 is best) on pulley, ball bearings, door rollers and hinge pins. Only a few drops are needed at each point.

Roller shafts should be free to slide back and forth in the roller bracket. Many manufacturers recommend general-purpose Lubriplate, available through automotive stores, since it's waterproof and unaffected by weather changes.

Another lubrication spot you shouldn't miss is inside the track where the rollers slide, especially around curved portions.

Should lubrication fail to solve the friction problem, check the door and door stops to see where and to what degree paint has been rubbed off. If you find evidence of excessive rubbing, you have two alternatives: You can move the stops away from the door if rubbing is localized in one or two areas, or you can move the door away from the stops if it is a general problem— that is, if rubbing occurs along most of the contact surface.

In the latter case, examine the hardware alongside of each track. Brackets holding the track away from the door may be spot-welded and not adjustable, or attached with bolts and fully adjustable.

If you have a door with adjustable brackets, loosen the bolts holding the track, pull the track toward you about ⅛ in. and tighten the nuts. This

will usually alleviate the problem. If you find friction localized to a few smaller areas, plane the stop to remove high spots.

It is important to have ¼ to ½ in. of side play between door and tracks at any position, open or closed. You should be able to float the door from side to side ¼ to ½ in. If not, the tracks may be too close to the door edge and bind the rollers.

To adjust, simply go back to the track brackets, back out the lags a few turns and move the tracks farther apart. Make sure tracks are vertical and evenly spaced by checking with a carpenter's level.

Spacing tracks too far apart is not a good idea. This could permit one side to reach higher than the other during open cycles. The condition, called "racking," wedges the door in the track and stops it.

The next problem is the door that is overweight due to moisture. Tip-offs to a moisture problem are surface checks and small cracks in panels. Springs can be adjusted to compensate for added weight, but during a dry spell you should thoroughly sand panels and repaint *both sides* with a quality exterior paint.

Adjusting for weight is done by putting more stretch in springs. But remember—do this only on extension-spring doors.

Most extension-spring doors are adjusted from the cable's dead end fastened to the hori-

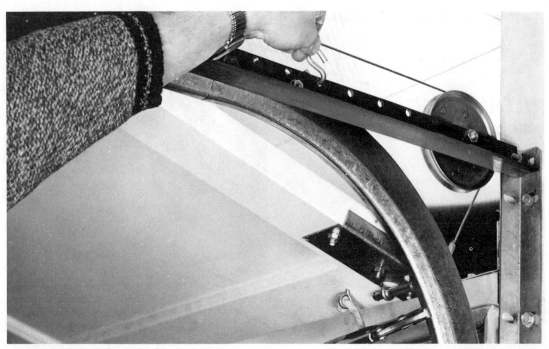

COMMON WAY to adjust spring tension is to change the S-hook placement. Vise clamps are used to hold the door.

zontal track reinforcing member near the door opening headers.

No matter how springs are adjusted, the door must be opened and propped, since springs will be detached and the door can fall. Prop the door open with clamps or by putting a strong ladder beneath it.

Many doors are anchored by S-hooks. To increase spring tension, first move one hook forward a few holes, then move the hook on the other side the same amount.

On some doors, spring adjustment is made by moving the back end of the extension spring over a notched bar. On still others, adjustments are made with an eyebolt and nut through the rear track hanger.

Next check for the proper balance point. With the bottom of the door 1 to 2 ft. off the floor, it should neither tend to raise nor fall by itself.

Above this position, a well-balanced door will tend to rise slowly by itself. Below it, the door should fall by itself.

If it's no longer possible to balance the door with the present springs, they should be replaced with stronger ones. If you can identify the make of door, you can probably get them from a dealer. If not, weigh the door (detach the springs and lower the door onto a bathroom scale placed under the center of the door).

You'll probably need help. A one-car garage door weighs up to 150 pounds; two-car sizes weigh 300 pounds and more. When you know the weight, ask a dealer to get workable springs.

To keep a working door troublefree, lubricate all moving and turning parts once every six months. At that time, tighten all loose bolts, check the cables for fraying or wear and make sure one hasn't slipped off its sheave.

Gardens and gardening

■ THERE ARE MANY reasons for having a home garden, not the least of which is the pure joy of growing wholesome fruits and vegetables. It's amazing what can be done with some seeds, soil, sun and water. Home gardening can easily provide a lifetime of quiet diversion.

A garden anywhere

Growing vegetables at home is not limited to people in the country. City dwellers have known for years it is possible to grow tomatoes, lettuce, peas, cucumbers and many other types of vegetables in containers. This can be done on window sills, terraces and balconies. While the harvest will not be as great as in a conventional garden, a variety of vegetables can be grown with a minimum of space and effort.

Home gardening is challenging. Transforming an otherwise unproductive section of your yard into a high-yield garden will test your skills and creativeness. The added bonus, of course, is a harvest all summer long.

When to begin

The home garden really begins in January, the month in which seed catalogs arrive in the mail. In these catalogs you'll find seeds that are time-proven and also those that are new for the upcoming season. This is the exciting time for planning the family garden—what to plant and where to plant it.

Even though it may be difficult to imagine a garden in bloom while snow is still flying, take advantage of the specials offered by seed catalogs and local garden centers early in the year.

How to begin

In almost any part of the country, it will be to your advantage to start your seeds indoors up to 60 days before you plan on setting the plants outdoors in a cold frame or directly in the garden.

Starting seeds indoors does not involve a lot of space or much in the way of special equipment. In fact, quite a few seeds can be germinated under a 2-ft.-wide by 4-ft.-long four-tube fluorescent light fixture. For best growing results you should use fluorescent light tubes designed for growing plants. These are usually available at garden supply shops.

Soil and light

In addition to a light fixture, you will need a special potting soil for starting your seeds. Many home gardeners use an equal mixture of perlite, peat moss, vermiculite and coarse sand. You can mix your own potting soil or purchase the ready-mixed type at your local garden supply shop.

There are also soil-less potting soils that are fun to experiment with.

The last items you will need for starting seeds indoors are plastic pots, trays and flats. While it is possible to start seeds indoors in almost any type of container, you will find it easier to grow uniform, robust plants with the more conventional containers used by commercial growers.

Since seeds will sprout and grow better in a warm environment, it is best to locate your grow lights in a warm area of your home. Almost anyplace that is not a high-traffic area will do. Some of the better choices include around the furnace, in a little-used closet or in an unoccupied but heated room. You can use almost any area that has a constant temperature and remains draft-free.

All fluorescent light fixtures are heavy and should be suspended from the ceiling properly. Ideally, ¼-in.-thick hooks or eyebolts should be screwed directly into the ceiling joists. If this is not possible, use suitable toggle bolts, such as those sold for hanging plants. Your seed sprouting and growing operation will be most efficient if the fluorescent fixture can be lowered and raised easily with the help of pulleys and rope.

ONE OF THE DIRECT BENEFITS of gardening is a bountiful harvest all summer long.

A WIDE VARIETY of vegetables can easily be grown in containers on a patio or apartment porch.

SMART GARDENERS get a jump on the season by starting seeds indoors under special grow lights.

Starting the seeds

The order in which plants should be started is closely related to the order in which plants will be set out in the garden. The first plants you will be starting include lettuce, spinach, broccoli, cauliflower, cabbage and parsley.

Begin planting by filling a container—such as a seed flat or plastic compartmentalized trays—

halfway with the special sprouting mixture. Next, drop individual seeds on top with suitable spacing between them. Then sprinkle ¼ to ½ in. of soil on top of the seeds. Water well and place the seed trays 4 to 6 in. below the grow lights. Make sure to label all containers with seed type and date of planting.

Growing plants will need about 18 hours of light and six hours of darkness a day. To ensure that your seedlings get the required lighting, it is wise to install an electric timer to turn your lights on and off at a predetermined time every day. Plug-in-type lamp timers are ideal for this and are well worth the modest cost.

Check and water your plants daily and, as the plants sprout and grow, move the grow lights up to maintain a 4 to 6-in. height above the seedlings.

Time to move outside

In about 6 to 8 weeks the plants should be tall and strong enough to be moved outdoors. If you have a cold frame, this is where the plants should go. If you don't have one, you can build one by following the directions given in this part of your Encyclopedia. The reason for transferring your seedlings to a cold frame is to make them hardy enough to withstand variable springtime temperatures.

SEEDLINGS MUST be hardened off in a cold frame before being transferred into the garden.

After a week or more of hardening-off, you can transfer the individual seedlings directly into the garden. The area that will receive the transplants should be well tilled and contain fertilizer or a layer of compost. Choose a cloudy or overcast day and water the seedlings well an hour or so before transplanting. This will minimize transplant shock. After the plants are set into the garden, protect them for the first few days from drying winds and baking sun. Use a little common sense here. If you see that the seedlings are drying up or withering, shelter them with cardboard windbreaks. The same holds true if the weatherman predicts a cool or frosty spring night.

Greenhouse starting

The most ideal situation for the home gardener is to have a greenhouse. On a small scale this can be a simple cold frame or a specially made hotbed. If resources and enthusiasm warrant, however, you will want to consider building a greenhouse or attaching a greenhouse unit to the south side of your home.

Starting seeds at home is just one way to get plants for your garden. A much simpler—although more expensive—way is to purchase your seedlings from a garden shop or nursery. By shopping early in the season, you should find a large selection of plants to choose from.

Getting the garden plot ready

As spring arrives, home gardening begins in earnest. Seeds can be sown directly into the garden for peas, spinach, broccoli and other cold-weather-loving plants. As the weather warms and the days lengthen, you can set out seedlings that require warmer weather such as tomatoes, summer squash, cucumbers and eggplant. Seeds for beans and corn are generally planted directly in garden soil rather than started beforehand.

This is an exciting and busy part of the growing season in the home garden. Before seeds or plants can be set into the garden, there is much to be done. Seed beds need to be tilled with the addition of compost and, if you are so inclined, commercial fertilizers and insecticides.

The compost heap

It's a fact that any garden will benefit from the addition of compost. Many home gardeners, however, tend to rely on commercial products more than the garden composter. There is a certain amount of work involved, to be sure, but the reward of natural fruits and vegetables is worth it for many so-called "organic gardeners."

A COMPOST BIN can be fancy like this commercial one, or you can make your own from concrete blocks or wood.

Compost is simply garden refuse that has been allowed to decay or decompose. Adding compost to any garden will enrich the soil more than any fertilizer will. Of greater importance, compost lightens garden soil and increases its overall ability to hold moisture. These are characteristics that are beneficial for strong root growth and plant development and that are not available in commercial fertilizers. One last point is the fact that compost is long-lived—gardens improve over time with the addition of compost, but commercial fertilizer must be reapplied at regular intervals.

A composter for your garden

Your garden composter need not be elaborate. There are, however, a few guidelines that can help you achieve success.

While it is possible to make garden compost by simply piling garden debris and letting decomposition take over, you will make compost faster in a more structured composter. Your composter can be as simple as a three-sided concrete block enclosure (stacked without mortar) about 3 ft. high. Or it can be as complex as a wooden or plastic composting bin arrangement. The key to success is access to the decaying compost pile.

THIS GARDEN TOOL has a variety of attachments that make it quite versatile in and around the home garden. Left to right: snow thrower, weeder/cultivator, string trimmer and edger.

Three-sided composters let you get at the pile regularly for turning with a pitchfork. This must be done to ensure that the pile is decaying uniformly.

Four factors determine the speed at which compost can be made: size of material being composted, heat, water and air circulation.

Material size will govern how quickly the compost will decay. Obviously it will take longer for a tree branch to become compost than it will for leaves. For this reason, you will want to chop or break up all garden waste before it is added to the compost pile. By using only small, uniform pieces of organic material, you can reasonably expect to make garden compost in a few weeks rather than a few months.

Heat is a natural byproduct of decomposition. The greatest heat is generated in the center of a compost pile. Since the edges decompose more slowly than the center, you must turn the outer edges—which dry out the quickest—into the center of the pile. This will ensure uniform decomposition. As a rule, more heat is generated during the warm months than during the cold months.

Water is critical to the decay process, so it is best to water the compost pile regularly. Each time you turn the pile or add new material, water should be added.

Air circulation is the last requirement for making compost quickly. While turning the compost pile often will introduce plenty of oxygen to the decaying mass, it is also a good idea to build your composter structure so that air can enter from all sides. If you build yours from blocks, lay them up so there are plenty of spaces between the joints—don't use mortar here. If you are considering building your composter from wood, also consider using chicken wire for the walls of the unit. This will allow plenty of air to get to the compost pile. Rigid plastic composting bins are made with adequate and well-spaced holes around the units.

Garden tools

There are a number of tools and machines that will take much of the hand labor out of gardening. As garden space and size increases, so does the need for more efficient tools to help make the work easier.

Tillers. One of the most laborious tasks in gardening is tilling the soil. Even if your garden is small, a power tiller will save hours of shovel work and do a much better job. Modern tillers will not only help prepare seed beds for planting but can also be used for working compost or fertilizer into the soil.

Wheelbarrows. Another task that can be made easier is moving soil or compost around the gar-

A POWER TILLER will save hours of shovel work and do a much better job.

number of excellent small tractors that are a good investment for the large garden. A variety of attachments, from mowers to tillers to snow blowers, are commonly available.

Chippers and shredders. While not essential, a chipper or shredder will make a number of garden chores easier. From cleaning up the garden in the spring and fall to converting tree branches into mulch, a garden chipper is a very handy tool around the garden.

Water supply. Water is one of the essentials for gardening on any scale. A water spigot that is within hose length of the garden will save you hours of extra steps. Of possible greater value is some type of irrigation or sprinkling system that you simply turn on to water your garden. A variety of systems are currently available for almost any garden size.

Hand tools. Although power tools and machines will make a lot of gardening work easier, the average-size garden will also require a selection of good hand tools to make various tasks easier to do. The list includes long-handled shovels, spades, pitchforks, hand trowels, cultivators, rakes and shears. Because there is such a vast selection of hand tools available, it may be difficult to choose the right tools for your needs. In general, though, it is wise to purchase the best tools you can afford. Quality hand tools not only help to get things done efficiently, they will also last for many years.

As you can well imagine, gardening requires time, patience and some sweat equity. In the long run, however, all gardeners feel that the time is well spent and the rewards many.

A CHIPPER or shredder is very useful for cleaning up and making uniform mulch.

den. A wheelbarrow will save hours of back-breaking work simply because it will let you move large amounts of heavy material easily. Wheelbarrows with inflatable tires are a better all-around choice than those with hard rubber tires.

Garden tractors. For really large gardens you might consider a garden tractor. There are a

A COMPLETE watering system will cut garden work in half and ensure your plants get the right amount of water.

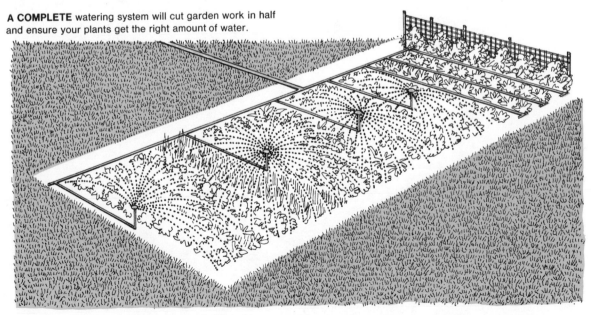

Cold frames let you get a jump on summer

■ THE MOST INEXPERIENCED wood-worker can build a cold frame suitable for the most experienced gardener. And if you like gardening, you'll find that a good cold frame is almost as useful as a small greenhouse, at a fraction of the cost.

The most versatile unit possible is really a combination of cold frame-hotbed. Separate storm sash and a center partition create two different areas. On the left is a cold frame heated by

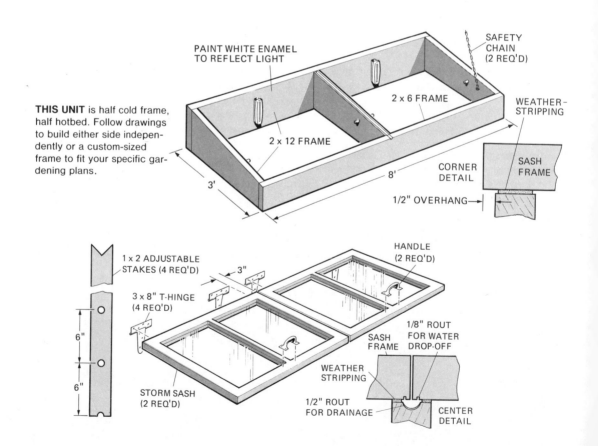

THIS UNIT is half cold frame, half hotbed. Follow drawings to build either side independently or a custom-sized frame to fit your specific gardening plans.

PAINT WHITE ENAMEL TO REFLECT LIGHT

SAFETY CHAIN (2 REQ'D)

2 x 6 FRAME

WEATHER-STRIPPING

2 x 12 FRAME

3'

8'

CORNER DETAIL

SASH FRAME

1/2" OVERHANG

1 x 2 ADJUSTABLE STAKES (4 REQ'D)

HANDLE (2 REQ'D)

3"

3 x 8" T-HINGE (4 REQ'D)

6"

6"

STORM SASH (2 REQ'D)

SASH FRAME

1/8" ROUT FOR WATER DROP-OFF

WEATHER STRIPPING

1/2" ROUT FOR DRAINAGE

CENTER DETAIL

ORGANIC HOTBED

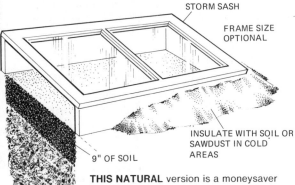

STORM SASH

FRAME SIZE OPTIONAL

INSULATE WITH SOIL OR SAWDUST IN COLD AREAS

9" OF SOIL

24" MANURE

THIS NATURAL version is a moneysaver if you can get manure from a local farm or stable. Low installation costs and no ongoing electricity costs at all will mean year-round vegetables and free flowers.

ELECTRIC HOTBED

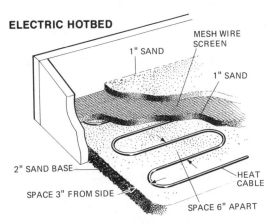

MESH WIRE SCREEN

1" SAND

1" SAND

2" SAND BASE

SPACE 3" FROM SIDE

HEAT CABLE

SPACE 6" APART

THIS YEAR-ROUND frame will do some gardening on its own by automatically controlling temperature level.

POLYETHYLENE FILM

STORM SASH

WOOD OR MASONRY FRAME

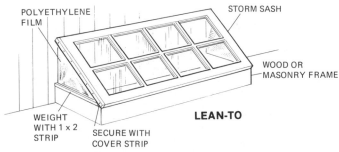

LEAN-TO

WEIGHT WITH 1 x 2 STRIP

SECURE WITH COVER STRIP

THIS SIMPLE cold frame is ideal for the south side of a barn or garage. You can use a wooden or masonry frame at the bottom and plastic sheets along the sides.

HEAVY WIRE

CLEAR FRAME

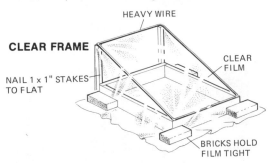

CLEAR FILM

NAIL 1 x 1" STAKES TO FLAT

BRICKS HOLD FILM TIGHT

NO-FRILLS model here, built with a minimum of time and money invested, will still get you satisfactory results.

PLASTIC WIRE GLASS

RAISED FRAME

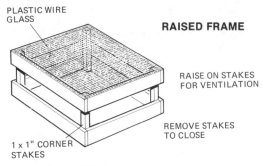

RAISE ON STAKES FOR VENTILATION

REMOVE STAKES TO CLOSE

1 x 1" CORNER STAKES

FOUR CORNER stakes are used to raise and lower this primitive but functional model. Construction is so simple that it makes a great project for a child.

YEAR-ROUND USES FOR COLD FRAMES

Early spring	Hardening-off plants—ease transition for young seedlings from greenhouse to garden.
Spring and summer	Seed sowing. Early start for hardy and half-hardy annuals and perennials.
Late spring and summer	Use sand or peat moss for propagation of cuttings.
Autumn	Seed sowing for dormant winter until early-spring germination.
Winter	Protection for newly started perennials. Growing tender bulbs. Storage for bulbs and plants to be forced.

VINYL DOME KIT ASSEMBLY

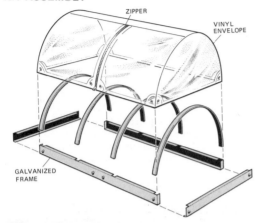

ZIPPER

VINYL ENVELOPE

GALVANIZED FRAME

SPRING WILL ARRIVE EARLY at your house with this growth dome. It provides 12 sq. ft. of heated space under a zippered vinyl envelope. The lightweight galvanized steel frame can be set up in 15 minutes and add 60 days to your growing season.

COLD FRAME VARIATIONS

TYPES
Wooden frame and sash
Masonry frame and sash
Wooden frame and plastic cover
Organic hotbed and conventional frame
Electric cable hotbed and conventional frame
Kits, growing dome
Lean-tos, wooden sash and frame

ACCESSORIES
Thermometer
Electric-heat cable element
Lath (snow fencing) for summer sash
Safety chains

the sun's rays. On the right is a year-round hotbed with an auxiliary heat supply. Most garden supply centers sell heat cable in different lengths that can be snaked over a two-inch sand base. The wire has a built-in sensing switch that automatically calls for heat if the in-frame temperature falls below 74°. You can build either side of this frame as an independent unit, or build the double sash size as all cold frame or all hotbed.

A lot for a little

Keep construction simple and efficient. Depending on how enterprising you are, you can use scrap wood and used storm sash to help keep the price tag for the complete setup below $100 and as low as $50. A cold frame is simply a slant-sided box with a transparent, hinged lid. Take a total dimension for the storm sash and make the frame ½ in. smaller on all four sides. This gives you a nice overhang to keep rainwater from dripping inside the frame. It also gives you a margin for error. If you're not an experienced woodworker, don't worry; you're not building a finished cabinet and a little enamel paint will make this unit look pretty good. Most garden books recommend cypress or redwood. But you can save some money with fir or any scrap wood on hand. Soak it well with two coats of a preservative and finish with two coats of exterior white enamel. Here are some tips for a successful installation:

● Locate with sash facing south.
● Provide a windbreak on north side.
● Make sure site is well drained.
● Install a thermometer.
● Maintain a temperature range of 40° to 100° F. (85° optimum).
● Keep airtight; use weatherstrip.
● Prevent sash blow-over with safety chains.

We've outlined different cold frames you can build down to the simplest and most temporary varieties. You can even dig a hole and spread plastic across the top secured with a few rocks.

365 days of summer

You'll get your investment back from the extra harvest of vegetables and flowers you can start ahead of schedule with a cold frame. Check the seasonal chart for year-round advantages of hotbeds. With either organic or electric versions you can have fresh chrysanthemums on a Thanksgiving table or a centerpiece of poinsettias for Christmas morning. The next stop in year-round gardening is a greenhouse.

Hotbed extends your growing season

■ IF YOU LOVE to raise your own vegetables, here's a way to continue growing them late into the fall. In the spring, you'll have your first garden-grown salad earlier than ever before.

The unit that performs these feats is called a "season-extender" because it extends both ends of the growing season. In the fall it will protect a patch of vegetables from the sudden killer frost that cuts off much of the garden production in its prime. And it will enable plants to tap the early sunshine of spring without the risk of being stunted by cold nights and the vagaries of spring weather. It uses hardware that even veteran gardeners may want to add to an existing hotbed, cold frame or greenhouse.

The main difference between the season-extender and a conventional cold frame is an automatically controlled lid to assure proper ventilation. The vent control eliminates the possibility of forgetting to raise or lower the lid. Ventilation is important because solar radiation, even when the air temperature outside is cool, can quickly raise the air temperature inside the season-extender to a dangerous level for young seed-

lings. The reverse is also true: A quick drop in air temperature can stunt seedlings.

The unit's walls are insulated with 1-in.-thick rigid Styrofoam panels to help retain heat. The lid is covered with a translucent plastic with closed-cell air bubbles that reduce the rate of heat loss through the lid by about 50 percent (over commonly used plastic films and window glass). Vinyl foam weatherstripping tape assures a tight seal between the lid and frame.

Knockdown design permits compact, off-season storage. Interlocking corner joints make the entire frame easy to take apart.

The season-extender can be used in at least four different ways. You can prolong the growing season of a specially planted, fall-winter crop if you build the bed for a late summer planting. Include rutabaga, bush beans, peas, radishes, lettuce, spinach and any other cool-weather crop that can fit within a 33 × 76-in. area. Plant the taller varieties in the back where they have more room to climb and will not block the sunlight from low-growing vegetables. When the nights begin to turn cold, position the season-extender

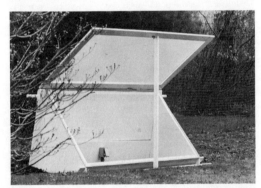

PROP WITH NOTCH holds lid open for watering or while you work in the bed. For extensive bed preparation, simply move the unit aside temporarily.

HOTBED OR "season-extender" holds seedlings for a typical 250-sq.-ft. vegetable garden, with room left over to start several trays of flowers.

NOTICE THAT IN this photo the south-facing unit has its lid partially opened. This is accomplished with an automatic vent control.

AS GROWING NEEDS change, it's a simple task to move the season-extender and use it in a new site.

AUTOMATIC vent control is activated by expansion of heat-sensitive compound inside cylinder.

PUSH ROD connects arm to lid bracket at ball-and-socket joint. Retaining cuff slides over the joint to secure it.

MATERIALS LIST—PM'S HOTBED

Key	Pcs.	Size and description (use)
A	2	¾" plywood—see plans (sides)
B	1	¾ x 38-5/16" x 7' plywood (back)
C	1	¾ x 7" x 7' plywood (front)
D	1	1½ x 1½ x 73" fir (mounting cleat for Thermofor)
E	2	1⅛"-dia. x 8' fir closet pole (lifters)
F	2	¾ x 4 x 46⅝" clear pine (lid framing)
G	2	¾ x 4 x 78" clear pine (lid framing)
H	1	4 x 7' (approx.) heavy duty, C-240, AirCap
I	2	¼ x 1⅛ x 41⅜" pine (lattice)
J	2	¼ x 1⅛ x 78½" pine (lattice)

Key	Pcs.	
K	3	1" x 2' x 8' Styrofoam (wall insulation)
L	2	3½ x 3½" loose-joint, loose-pin steel hinges
M	1	Thermofor unit assembly, mounting hardware
N	1	¾ x 4" x 6' plywood (prop)

Misc: 6 2" No. 10 fh wood screws; 16 ¾" No. 8 fh wood screws; ⅜" staples; 1¼" brads; Dow's Mastic 11; resorcinol glue; ½ x ¾" x 21' foam tape weatherstripping; ext. white gloss, alkyd or urethane type paint; ext. white gloss latex paint.
Note: All plywood is ¾" AC or CD exterior grade.

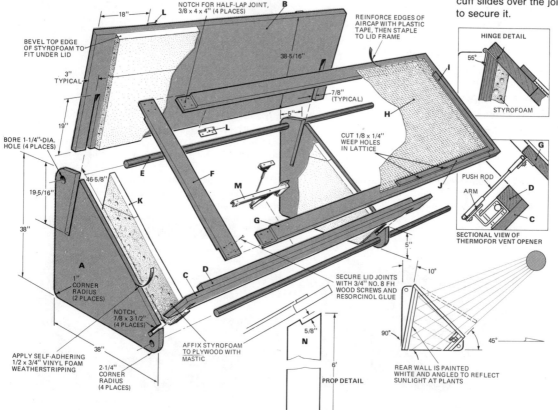

HOW TO MAKE A PERMANENT HOTBED INSTALLATION

If you don't have an outdoor receptacle, think about installing one for use with your hotbed—and for any other yard tasks requiring electrical power. If you're locating the unit near the house, choose a south-facing wall and mount the outlet on the structure. If installation is away from the house, mount it on a pipe as shown below. Dig a trench and bury UF cable; pass cable through a hole in the basement wall or header joist. Connect circuit to the nearest inside junction box that can handle additional load.

The National Electric Code requires ground-fault circuit interrupter (GFCI) protection for all outdoor installations. GFCIs are available at electrical supply houses and must be installed according to manufacturer's directions. Check with your town electrical inspector before you begin. Call in a licensed electrician if you doubt your wiring ability.

Laying soil-heating cables

Begin by digging a 10-in.-deep pit with the same dimensions as the bottom

of your season-extender. Spread a 4-in.-thick layer of pea gravel and sand. Then make an insulated floor with the leftover scraps of Styrofoam. Attach heating cables (see below) with thermostat to insulation and cover with 1 in. of a soil-humus mixture, hardware cloth and more planting medium until the pit is full. Grade the planting surface slightly to slope southward.

PVC MAY BE used for conduit. To join, clean off dust and burrs, pretest fit. Give ¼-in. twist after applying cement.

USE PLASTIC tape or insulated tacks to hold soil-heating cables in parallel loops. Maintain 3-in. intervals.

COVER HEATING wires with 1-in. layer of sand or soil: add hardware cloth for protection from misdirected spade.

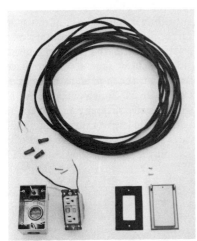

FOR SAFE yard/garden outlet you need: a UL-listed outdoor junction box, G.F.C.I. receptacle, weatherproof coverplate with gasket and direct-burial cable.

OUTDOOR RECEPTACLE INSTALLATION

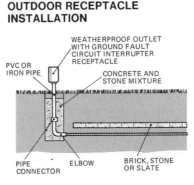

WEATHERPROOF OUTLET WITH GROUND FAULT CIRCUIT INTERRUPTER RECEPTACLE
PVC OR IRON PIPE
CONCRETE AND STONE MIXTURE
PIPE CONNECTOR
ELBOW
BRICK, STONE OR SLATE

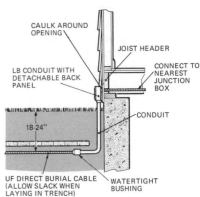

CAULK AROUND OPENING
JOIST HEADER
LB CONDUIT WITH DETACHABLE BACK PANEL
CONNECT TO NEAREST JUNCTION BOX
CONDUIT
18-24"
UF DIRECT BURIAL CABLE (ALLOW SLACK WHEN LAYING IN TRENCH)
WATERTIGHT BUSHING

over the bed and see how much longer this patch will produce.

In the spring, use the unit as a hotbed to start seedlings early. A hotbed requires a heat source

other than the sun, such as decomposing manure or soil-heating cables. Cables last many years and produce even, thermostatically controlled heat.

Instead of a hotbed application, you may choose to make the most of the frame's portability by using it as a "direct-plant" cold frame in the spring. Put it in the garden as soon as the ground can be prepared and sow hardy crops like spinach, lettuce, cabbage, broccoli, cauliflower, Brussels sprouts and radishes. When the patch is well established, move the extender and use it to give a bed of less hardy plants like tomatoes, zucchini, melons or peppers an early start.

Finally, an extender abutted to the south wall of a house and provided with soil-heating cables can be used as a miniature greenhouse to winter over many house, patio and yard plants. If your climate is mild, you may be able to use the season-extender to continue growing vegetables throughout the winter. For cold-weather use, disconnect the automatic vent and provide a glass or clear plastic lid in addition to the plastic bubble film material. The rigid lid material is required to protect the plastic bubble film from tearing under snow loads.

Begin building the season-extender by cutting out the four walls and prop from two 4 × 8-ft. sheets of plywood. Lay out completely before you start cutting. Cut notches as shown in the plans, using a handsaw or circular saw to make parallel cuts and a chisel to knock out waste. Bore holes for the lifters and use a sabre saw to round off the corners. Next, center the thermostatically controlled motor for mounting cleats (D) on the front wall and fasten with 2-in. No. 10 flathead wood screws.

To insulate, first transpose the dimensions of the inside wall surfaces onto the Styrofoam. Use the inner edges of the notches as guides. Shorten the length of the back sections by 2 in. in order to form corner butt joints. Use a hollow-ground blade in a sabre saw for cutting the Styrofoam. Insulating the low, front wall is optional—in any case, don't allow it to interfere with the operation of the lid's motor unit.

Next, build the lid frame. You can rip 4-in. boards from one 12-ft. length of 1 × 10. Cut half-lap joints and assemble as shown.

A protective finish on all wood members is extremely important. Fill all gaps and knot holes with wood putty and exterior paint. Sand and recoat with paint every other year or as needed.

The Styrofoam insulation should also be painted. It deteriorates after prolonged exposure to sunlight. Use *water-based* exterior latex paint only. (Solvent-based coatings will dissolve insulation.) White gloss is best for maximum reflection of sunlight off the back and sides, and onto the plants.

Before slipping the unit together, use a candle stub to apply a coating of wax inside notches to prevent sticking. With walls assembled, affix pieces of rigid insulation to the plywood walls with a suitable water-based adhesive. *Do not use petroleum-based adhesives.*

Assemble the lid with screens and resorcinol glue. The bubble film should be installed with the bubbles down.

You may substitute a double layer of transparent plastic film for the bubble film. In either case, keep the edges from tearing by lining the inside edges of the lid with plastic tape, stapled in place. Nail lattice strips over the tape and staples using 1¼-in. brads 16 in. apart. Finish construction by installing hinges, weatherstripping and the motor unit. You might use the leftover plywood to build an inside divider so one section can be used with heating cables and the other without, if desired.

Gardening aids you can build

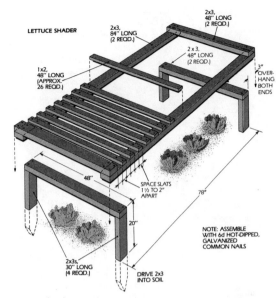

LETTUCE SHADER

2x3, 84" LONG (2 REQD.)

2x3, 48" LONG (2 REQD.)

2 x 3, 48" LONG (2 REQD.)

1x2, 48" LONG (APPROX 26 REQD.)

3" OVER-HANG BOTH ENDS

48"

SPACE SLATS 1½ TO 2" APART

78"

NOTE: ASSEMBLE WITH 6d HOT-DIPPED, GALVANIZED COMMON NAILS

20"

2x3s, 30" LONG (4 REQD.)

DRIVE 2x3 INTO SOIL

Lettuce shader

The lettuce shader does a perfect job of partially shading lettuce from the sun. This minimizes leaf burn and produces a more bountiful crop. If you build it of No. 2 common pine and treat it with wood preservative, it will last for years.

Since the slat assembly is not attached to the legs, you can store it nearly flat against a wall.

The shader shown has 1 × 2 slats spaced 1½ to 2 in. apart. These are secured by 6d hot-dipped galvanized nails to a base of 2 × 3 rails and end pieces. You can also use 2 × 4s.

Cut stake joints on the legs as shown. Secure the legs to their cross members. Apply a wood preservative.

A pair of shading units can share a common (center) leg unit if each shader is set to occupy just half the crosspiece width. This leaves a lip upon which the next shader can rest.

Potting bench

The simple but sturdy potting bench is built to withstand strenuous daily use. Plans are for a version to suit a home gardener's needs and space limitations. A garden tool board and a top shelf for parking flowerpots during work sessions have been added.

The bench is framed with pressure-treated 2 × 4s; work and storage surfaces are 1 × 6s. Or you can use common pine for the frame and work surfaces. If you opt for the latter, coat all surfaces of these members with a wood preservative several hours before you assemble the parts. Give the bench a second coat.

You can use exterior plywood for bench shelf, sides and back. The board to hold tools is perforated hardboard fitted with tool-holding hardware.

Cut frame members for the deck. Hold parts together temporarily with bar clamps. Check corners with a large square; adjust if needed. Then bore pilot holes for nails to prevent the wood from splitting. Use resorcinol glue and nails to assemble parts.

Cut the 1 × 6s for the work surface and the lower storage shelf to length. Cut the notches for the legs in two shelf members. Bore pilot holes and nail the work top in place.

Cut the plywood sides and back. The sides taper in height from 21 in. in back to 7 in. in front. Glue and nail the back and sides to the bench top and to each other.

Cut the upper shelf to size and bore the optional flowerpot holes. You can make these using a fly cutter in the drill press, but clamp the shelf firmly to the press table on both sides of the cutter. Or you can make the circular cuts with a sabre saw.

The bench legs are cut to length and the notches are cut. You can make the internal notches with a sabre saw and chisel. Or use a radial-arm saw in this manner: Mark for notch width and depth on the face of the leg and align the notch (waste) area with the saw blade. Adjust the blade to notch depth. Make successive overlapping passes with the blade. Clean using a chisel.

Rest the bench top bottom side up. Position the back legs; bore pilot holes, and glue and nail the legs in place.

Rotate the bench onto its front assembly and install the front legs in the same manner. Let the glue dry for 24 hours. Next, cut the lower frame members to length. Test-assemble using clamps, and bore pilot holes after checking that the frame is square. Then secure the parts with glue and nails.

Finally, cut out parts for the tool board. Glue and nail the frame together with 4d nails and set aside. Bore lead holes and fasten the cleats to the

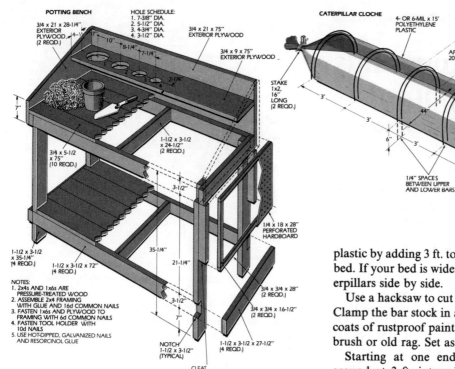

POTTING BENCH

HOLE SCHEDULE:
1. 7-3/8" DIA.
2. 5-1/2" DIA.
3. 4-3/4" DIA.
4. 3-1/2" DIA.

3/4 x 21 x 28-1/4"
EXTERIOR
PLYWOOD
(2 REQD.)

3/4 x 21 x 75"
EXTERIOR PLYWOOD

3/4 x 9 x 75"
EXTERIOR PLYWOOD

3/4 x 5-1/2
x 75"
(10 REQD.)

1-1/2 x 3-1/2
x 24-1/2"
(2 REQD.)

1/4 x 18 x 28"
PERFORATED
HARDBOARD

1-1/2 x 3-1/2
x 35-1/4"
(4 REQD.)

1-1/2 x 3-1/2 x 72"
(4 REQD.)

35-1/4"

21-1/4"

3/4 x 3/4 x 28"
(2 REQD.)

3/4 x 3/4 x 16-1/2"
(2 REQD.)

1-1/2 x 3-1/2 x 27-1/2"
(4 REQD.)

NOTCH
1-1/2 x 3-1/2"
(TYPICAL)

CLEAT,
1-1/2 x 2-1/4 x 23-3/4"
(2 REQD.)

NOTES:
1. 2x4s AND 1x6s ARE PRESSURE-TREATED WOOD
2. ASSEMBLE 2x4 FRAMING WITH GLUE AND 16d COMMON NAILS
3. FASTEN 1x6s AND PLYWOOD TO FRAMING WITH 6d COMMON NAILS
4. FASTEN TOOL HOLDER WITH 10d NAILS
5. USE HOT-DIPPED, GALVANIZED NAILS AND RESORCINOL GLUE

CATERPILLAR CLOCHE

4- OR 6-MIL x 15'
POLYETHYLENE
PLASTIC

1/4"-DIA. x 80"
HOT-ROLLED
STEEL BAR
(10 REQD.)

UPPER-
LEVEL BAR

GATHER
PLASTIC AT END
AND TIE
WITH TWINE

LOWER-
LEVEL
BAR

STAKE
1x2,
16"
LONG
(2 REQD.)

APPROX.
20"

1/4" SPACES
BETWEEN UPPER
AND LOWER BARS

legs with 10d nails. Bore lead holes and fasten the perforated hardboard to the bench with 6d common nails. Apply veneer edge tape to exposed edges, if desired, using contact cement.

Caterpillar cloche

The caterpillar cloche adds a season extender to your garden. You can assemble it in several hours with tape measure, hacksaw, paint brush, scissors or knife, and hammer.

Materials you'll need include ¼-in.-dia. hot-rolled steel bar, 4- or 6-mil polyethylene plastic, rustproof paint, two 16-in. wood stakes and twine. Steel bar is sold in 20-ft. lengths (check the classified directory under "Steel distributors and warehouses"). The cloche shown covers a 40-in.-wide × 12-ft. planting bed. You'll need four bars to cut ten 80-in. lengths. For beds of other dimensions, allow two arched bars for every 3 ft. of garden bed.

The cloche shown requires a 4 × 15-ft. piece of plastic. For other sizes, figure the amount of

plastic by adding 3 ft. to the length of the growing bed. If your bed is wider than 4 ft., place two caterpillars side by side.

Use a hacksaw to cut the bars to 80-in. lengths. Clamp the bar stock in a vise to cut it. Apply two coats of rustproof paint to the bars using a paint brush or old rag. Set aside to dry.

Starting at one end of the bed, mark the ground at 3-ft. intervals; you'll insert the steel bars at these points. Mark along one side of the bed, then along the other.

Push a steel bar for the lower level of bars about 6 in. into the ground. If it doesn't stand by itself, push it deeper. Straddling the bed, grip the top of the bar and slowly bend it toward the marked spot on the opposite side of the bed. Then push the end 6 in. into the soil. Repeat on the lower-level bars.

Unroll and spread out the polyethylene plastic and cut it to size. Lay the plastic over the support bars. Gather the last 18 in. of plastic at one end and tie it with twine; repeat at the other end.

Cut the wood stakes to 16-in. lengths. Tie one end of the plastic around a stake and hammer the stake in place. Then tie the plastic to the other stake and pull the plastic tight before hammering the stake.

Insert the upper level of steel bars directly over the lower ones, leaving ¼ in. between them so the plastic slides freely for covering or uncovering.

The plastic skin should open rolltop-desk-fashion. Pull the plastic up about 2 ft. at each support; then continue to pull it to reveal the entire bed.

Keep varmints out of your vegetable patch

■ FIRST, LET'S DETERMINE just who your enemies are out on the "garden front." Here's a rundown on 10 of the most common pests and the most effective means you can use to discourage their attacks.

1. Moles

Burrowing beneath the surface of the soil, moles create their labyrinths of interconnecting travel tubes. Actually, they aren't after your plants. They want a hearty meal of worms and insects. But in their searching and tunneling, they can dislodge more plant roots in a minute than healthy seed can sprout in a month.

Agricultural and conservation authorities say the best mole control is accomplished by trapping. Choker traps and harpoon traps have proven adequate for the task. The best time to trap is in early spring when the first mole ridges appear.

Find the active mole runways by mashing down the ridges where the runs have entered the edge of your garden. Watch to see which ones the moles will raise again. You can assume that the rebuilt runways are in regular use, so start your trapping there. Install either the harpoon or choker-type trap at those points according to instructions that come with the devices. Such traps are easy to set and are available at hardware stores and garden supply centers.

2. Cottontails

And now for another "enemy." He's bouncing along the edge of your garden, flashing a fuzzy white tail, and he's looking for just one thing—a free meal, courtesy of you and your garden.

Rabbits do more damage to the actual plants than do moles, for a cottontail likes to chomp on stems and leaves of vegetables.

So here's your battle plan: Try wire guards around individual plants if you have the room for them. Hardware cloth, also known as chicken wire, works well. Make the guards high enough so that a rabbit can't stand up on his hind legs and reach his lunch.

Repellents can help you cut damage, too. Area or odor repellents, though, are not very effective. These might include mothballs, creosote oil and similar substances. Apparently a rabbit's "taster" is more sensitive than his "smeller," for taste repellents are much more effective in sending him scooting.

During the growing season, you can discourage rabbits by spraying nicotine sulfate on your garden. Add half a teaspoon of 40-percent nicotine sulfate to one quart of water. You may also wish to try one, or several, of the commercially prepared repellents that are available through garden supply stores. Some of these are:

No Nib'l can be dusted on or it can be sprayed. The can has a shaker top for dusting. If you want to spray, mix the contents of the 6-ounce can with 2½ gallons of water.

Improved Z.I.P. is sprayed on. Use one quart of the material to 7 quarts of water.

Arasan 75 is another spray-on repellent. Add one quart Rhoplex AG-33 or Latex 512R to 14½ quarts of water. Mix thoroughly with one pound of Arasan 75. Strain and then stir frequently while using.

Arasan 42-S sprayed on works well. Add one pint Rhoplex AG-33 or Latex 512R to 7 quarts of water. Mix thoroughly with one pint of Arasan 42-S. Mix only enough repellent for immediate use as the solids settle after standing several days and you'll have trouble getting them to resuspend. It may be necessary to spray frequently in order to cover new growth.

Caution: Do not treat your vegetables after edible portions have started to form on beans, cabbages, lettuce and the like as the repellents may be caught in them and retained. If they are, more than the rabbits will be "repelled."

Make life tough on your rabbit-type moochers. Cleanly cultivate the area around your garden, removing brush piles and heavy wood growth. This takes away a rabbit's natural cover and tends to reduce his desire to hang around for a handout.

A final weapon in your rabbit arsenal is a good box trap. This is a humane method because you don't kill the animal. You take the trap far away in the woods and release your catch without harm.

3. Gophers

If you're in gopher country, you know these small ground squirrels "go fer" roots, fruits, seeds and leafy garden vegetation. Their favorite food-hunting sport is digging up recently planted vegetable seeds. They seem to like sweet corn best.

Control measures include the use of poisoned bait. If you expect to use this tricky stuff, you'll be wise to talk to your local agricultural extension service personnel (state college of agriculture people) for advice on handling. When *correctly* distributed, there is little hazard to beneficial wildlife or livestock.

Ground squirrels can be gassed with calcium cyanide, but this, too, is a highly dangerous substance and should be used only with extreme caution. It releases deadly hydrocyanic acid into their burrows (upon contact with air) and that's a powerful gas.

Trapping is your safest method for eliminating ground squirrels. Either No. O steel traps or regular wooden-based rat traps can be placed in shallow pits near burrow entrances. Lure your victim to the traps by sprinkling small amounts of grain on the thin layer of dirt covering the trap trigger.

4. Raccoons

Raccoons come all dressed for the part, as they make like robbers and steal from your growing garden. They like corn, especially when the ears are in the milk stage.

Raccoons are easy to catch with traps that don't kill. However, if you want to go after them with a vengeance you can use No. 2 double-coil-spring fox traps. Several kinds of "sets" are successfully used, but the "dirt hole" is probably the best.

Set the trap about a ½ inch below the ground, one or two feet from the side of a coon trail alongside the garden. Cover lightly with sifted soil. Cover the trap pan with a piece of tissue or canvas to prevent dirt from getting under it and locking it open. Dig a small hole about 6 inches deep and 3 inches across at a slant just behind the trap. Raccoons are attracted to such a set by the use of a gland lure in the dirt hole in winter and early spring and by the use of a food lure the rest of the year. Both lures are available from trapping equipment suppliers.

You can also try using a steel-cage live-trap, baiting it with some freshly cut corn. If your coons are familiar with human scent, you may catch the culprit this way. In his trap, transport him far enough away so that when you release him, unharmed, he'll have to find someone else's garden to plunder.

Ordinary fencing will not keep raccoons from your garden. If they can't go under it or through it, they'll wiggle themselves over it. However, since raccoons prefer late lunches—in the dark—you can sometimes deter them by hanging some lights around the garden. The more movement the lights have, the better, but don't count on this method for 100-percent success.

Oil of mustard is obnoxious to animals—as well as to most gardeners. If you can stand the stuff, you can mix one ounce of oil of mustard and one ounce of household detergent with one gallon of water. Spray applications at three-day intervals may be necessary to stop persistent raccoon raids. Don't spray directly on sweet corn ears, but treat the ground around the stalks late in the evening.

5. Opossums

Opossums will eat practically anything. If they're plaguing your garden, you'll have to trap them. Repellents seem to have little effect on these night prowlers. No. 1½ or No. 2 steel traps, set in natural or artificial openings in their den areas, will "stop them in their tracks." For bait, use meat scraps, fish or moist dog food.

6. Pets

Ordinary domestic animals can wreak havoc in your garden when the neighbor's pooch chases your cat through your pumpkin patch. Control? Probably a strong fence, or maybe a permanent leash for both of the villains.

7. Turtles

Box turtles thrive on tomatoes, especially those

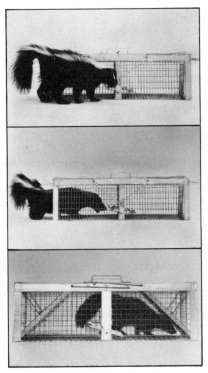

METAL TRAPS come in sizes that will accommodate anything from a mouse to a fox.

SIMPLE BOX TRAP for rabbits and other small animals can be made from scrap wood.

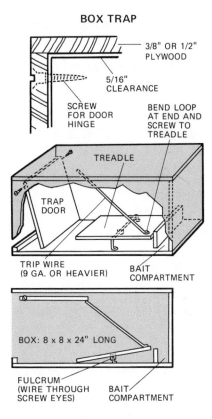

BOX TRAP

3/8" OR 1/2" PLYWOOD

5/16" CLEARANCE

SCREW FOR DOOR HINGE

BEND LOOP AT END AND SCREW TO TREADLE

TREADLE

TRAP DOOR

TRIP WIRE (9 GA. OR HEAVIER)

BAIT COMPARTMENT

BOX: 8 x 8 x 24" LONG

FULCRUM (WIRE THROUGH SCREW EYES)

BAIT COMPARTMENT

found lying directly on the ground. You can foil this mobile-homed nomad of nature by driving four or five-foot stakes alongside tomato plants and then carefully tying the plants up to keep the tomatoes off the ground.

8. Squirrels

Red and gray squirrels have been known to nibble at garden vegetables, too. Try tying aluminum pie tins to stakes so they flash and clatter in the wind. Only the most persistent, most hungry squirrel will risk his bushy tail amid such a clanking commotion.

9. Deer

If deer in your area are proving themselves to be garden pests, you'll find an effective control (probably in conjunction with a tall fence) to be bone tar oil, an odor-producing chemical. It is sold under various trade names. Follow the manufacturer's directions carefully for mixing and application.

It is best to make your first application before deer develop a habit of tasting your garden's offerings. Subsequent applications should be made monthly. If deer are already helping themselves

at your smorgasbord, you may have to mix a solution stronger than normal.

10. Birds

Not all attacks on your garden will come from enemy forces moving over the ground. You may find your tomatoes the target for airborne action from birds. Scare-type devices will work to keep birds away sometimes, but not always. Sticky repellents have been used along with plastic twirlers, cloth strips and other moving objects and are fairly effective for small areas. The best, most positive protection comes from netting that will completely enclose your crop.

Authorities say, however, that effective bird control depends on three prime factors:

1. Timing: Control measures should be started at the first indication of damage.

2. Persistence: As long as nature's air force attacks (grackles, starlings, blackbirds, cowbirds and sometimes even woodpeckers), your garden is vulnerable, so control measures should be used.

3. Diversification: No single method is always satisfactory: Various devices must be used in combination and their placement frequently shifted.

Transplanting tips

■ THERE ARE SEVERAL KINDS of transplanting, but certain guidelines apply to them all. For instance, *correct planting time is extremely important, even critical*. If you do not know the correct planting time in your area for a certain plant, by all means check your catalogs or call a reputable local nursery. *Transplant only at the optimum time*. If possible, choose a cool and cloudy or rainy day without wind.

Select the sturdiest and best-shaped specimens for transplanting. Dig holes for them that are straight-sided and are deep and wide enough to accommodate the roots without crowding. Expose the roots to the air no longer than is absolutely necessary because in some cases just a few minutes of exposure is too much. Protect the roots, if the soil falls off, by putting them into water or a moistened plastic bag. Trim off broken or bruised roots with a sharp knife or shears.

For best results, prepare a good soil mixture to surround the transplant. Dig in humus like peat moss, rotted manure or compost to lighten the soil and make it hold more water. The humus will encourage the young plant—whether a tomato vine or a tree—to root quickly and well. One caution—if you use fertilizer, place it in the dirt well beneath roots or stem, so it does not touch them.

Most plants should be set the same depth as

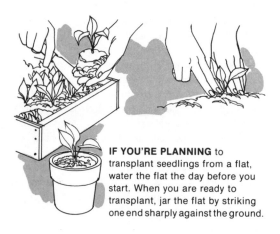

IF YOU'RE PLANNING to transplant seedlings from a flat, water the flat the day before you start. When you are ready to transplant, jar the flat by striking one end sharply against the ground.

they were growing originally. Firm the soil gently around the roots but don't pack it in. Make a surface basin, and water it thoroughly to settle the soil. Around a tree this basin should be extended each year as the roots spread.

If you have an especially large, delicate transplant, you may be able to ease the shock of transfer by a two-stage process. A few days before the actual transplanting, prune the roots by driving a spade down in a circle around the plant. This will give the plant some time to recover from the initial shock.

Balled, burlapped and potted plants

Many trees and shrubs, including evergreens, are sold balled and burlapped. The nursery encases the entire root system in burlap and ties it with twine. In handling such plants: 1. Do not bump or jar the root ball, which can cause the soil to separate from the roots. For the same reason: 2. Do not use the trunk as a handle, even though it invites you to do so. If the weight is not too great, cradle the root ball in your arms. Using a sling of stout cloth, two people can carry a heavier plant. If necessary, a third can support the trunk.

Dig the planting hole *about twice the diameter of the root ball,* and deep enough so there will be 8 or 10 in. of loosened soil under the ball. That loose soil is very important. Set the plant so the top of the ball is just a bit higher—say, half an inch—than the surrounding surface. This will allow for settling. Now split the burlap and fold it

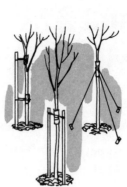

back from the top but leave it on the rest of the ball. It will not hurt the plant, and will gradually rot away. Fill the hole with enriched topsoil, firming it with a tamper made from a 2x4, and water thoroughly. Make sure that the plant stands straight and its best side faces in the direction you want.

If your tree or shrub comes in a large pot, allow the soil to dry out somewhat before planting. Then turn the pot on its side and grasp the trunk. Pull gently as you tap around the rim of the pot. The whole soil mass will slip out and the plant then can be handled in much the same way as a balled and burlapped one.

Bare roots and 'canned' plants

During winter and early spring you can buy bareroot dormant trees and shrubs that are less expensive than plants in containers sold months later. If the ground is still frozen when you buy bare-root plants, heel them in until you can plant them.

In setting a bare-root plant, form a mound in the hole, using the native soil from the hole mixed with an equal amount of organic material such as peat moss. Spread the bare roots over this mound. Fill the hole, and water as with other plants.

Plants are sold in cans in some areas. After preparing the planting hole, use tin shears to cut off the can (many nurseries will slit the can for you). Make two cuts directly opposite each

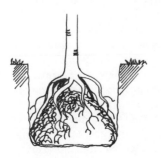

other. While supporting the trunk, slip the can off the soil mass. Loosen the roots a bit, and set the plant. Be sure you use gloves in handling the can, as the cut edges are very sharp.

After trees and shrubs arrive

Sometimes an emergency arises. You may not be able to set out your plants as soon as you get them. In that case, heel them in. In particular, this applies to bare-root plants.

Newly transplanted trees may need helpful support. *Before transplanting the tree,* drive a single stake 6 to 8 ft. long and 1½ to 2 in. in diameter into the transplanting hole. Position the stake on the same side of the tree as the prevailing winds. For even more support two stakes, or a combination of stakes and guy wires, may be used. Use turnbuckles to keep any wires taut. And never loop wire directly around the trunk; use cloth ties or rubber against the bark. Sometimes the trunk of a tree is wrapped with tarred paper. This conserves moisture and prevents sunscald.

Bulbs and perennials

When you transplant perennials or bulbs, resist the temptation to do it just after the plants have bloomed, while foliage is still green. That is the time the bulbs are being nourished by the leaves and developed for next year. Instead, you can fold the foliage and tie it neatly with a rubber band, then plant a shallow annual to cover the leaves when they turn brown, after which bulbs can be dug and stored.

In general, it is best to plant summer and fall-blooming perennials in the spring and to plant kinds that bloom in very early spring and summer in the autumn. But transplant irises in June or July, right after they bloom.

Bountiful harvest with little work

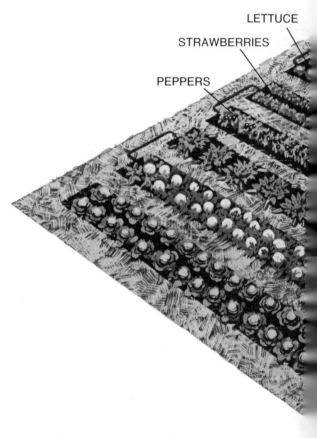

LETTUCE
STRAWBERRIES
PEPPERS

■ HOW WOULD you like to grow a vegetable garden in which there are no weeds and no serious pest damage; where there is no digging after the first year and no manual watering? Yet, despite the minimal effort, the garden is highly productive, beginning early in the season.

A system of mulching that utilizes black plastic prevents weeds from growing. After the first year's digging to make raised growing rows, simply replenish the soil each year with compost. Instead of hosing or sprinkling, inexpensive drip irrigation makes watering automatic and efficient. Organic pest controls keep pests away.

The garden shown is 15x41 ft. You can dig your own site in spring and divide it into 2-ft.-wide by 4 to 5-in.-high raised rows, with 1-ft.-wide walkways. To raise the rows, rake the soil from the walkways or use compost. Level them on top.

Midway at the garden edge lay two 150-ft. lengths of polyflex drip irrigation hose with 2-ft. emitter spacings, along the middle of the rows, in

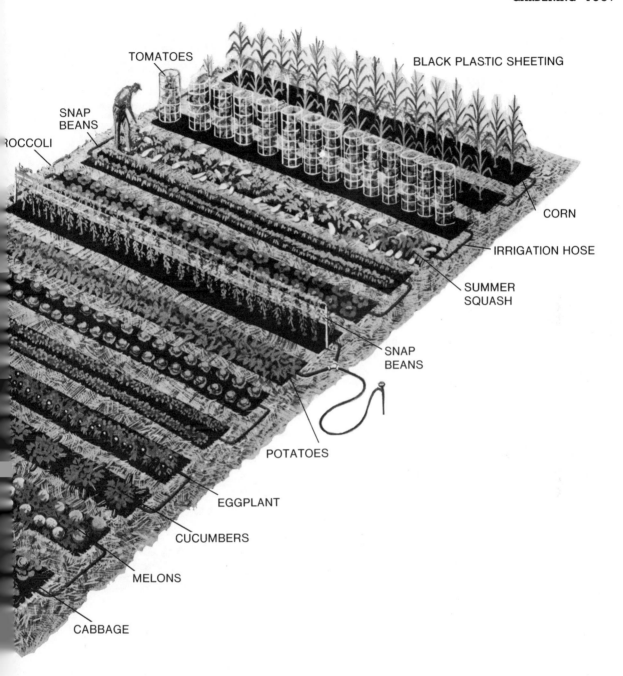

TOMATOES

SNAP
BEANS

BROCCOLI

BLACK PLASTIC SHEETING

CORN

IRRIGATION HOSE

SUMMER
SQUASH

SNAP
BEANS

POTATOES

EGGPLANT

CUCUMBERS

MELONS

CABBAGE

opposite directions, snaked up one row and down the next. Connect the two hoses to a water spigot with a Y-valve. Every inch of row can be watered in 30 minutes.

Next, cover the raised beds with 3-ft.-wide rolls of black plastic, leaving a 1- to 2-in. lip along the walkway for soil anchorage. On the walkways place layers of newspapers, then pine needles, to form an impenetrable, attractive mulch. Cut holes in the plastic for seeds and transplants.

Leave the plastic in place all winter—it warms the soil early and prevents insects. In spring, replace the plastic after conditioning the soil.

To control pests, use a rotenone-pyrethrum or a diatomaceous earth-pyrethrum mixture insecticide. Both are made from natural compounds that leave no residue. Apply insecticide *early* to keep pests at bay. Also, clean up dead vegetation in fall to prevent pests from wintering.

To maintain nutrient levels, use compost with bone meal added. For tomatoes, peas and heavy feeders, also use liquid fertilizer.

Grow a vegetable bonanza in a small plot

■ IN GARDENING, the magic words are *sunlight* and *nutrients*. Your first step is to pick a spot for the garden in full day-long sun, where the roots of large trees are not consuming the lion's share of the soil's nutrients and moisture. A plot of only 6 by 15 feet—basic size discussed in this article—can produce plenty of food for your table. If you have more area, better still.

Fertilizers

Today's vegetables, hybridized for rapid growth and high yield, need help in the form of extra nutrients. You give them the needed boost with a complete fertilizer, formulated for vegetables. Most garden stores have such fertilizers in five-pound boxes carrying designations such as 5-10-5, 5-10-10, 10-15-10.

The numbers denote percentages of nitrogen, phosphate and potash (in that order). Normally, before planting you'll want to work into the soil about five pounds of 5-10-5 per 100 square feet after each four weeks of growth. Use smaller amounts if you're working with a fertilizer of higher concentration.

In the growing season, never let fertilizer remain on leaves or within an inch of plant stems. It's wise to rake the soil lightly after each application and then give the whole garden a good watering.

Fertilizers that are completely soluble in water are excellent for use during the growing season. Used as directed, they will not burn leaves.

Compact soil

Soil too tightly packed inhibits root development. During rainy periods it will waterlog, cutting off normal aeration both to the roots and to beneficial microorganisms. In dry periods, it will cake on top so that water from the hose runs off or forms puddles while the soil beneath remains dry. Eventually, the soil may crack under the hot sun and cause damage to tender root growth.

The remedy is to work into the soil (up to one-third the volume of the soil in your garden) compost mixed with sand or perlite. This will allow drainage.

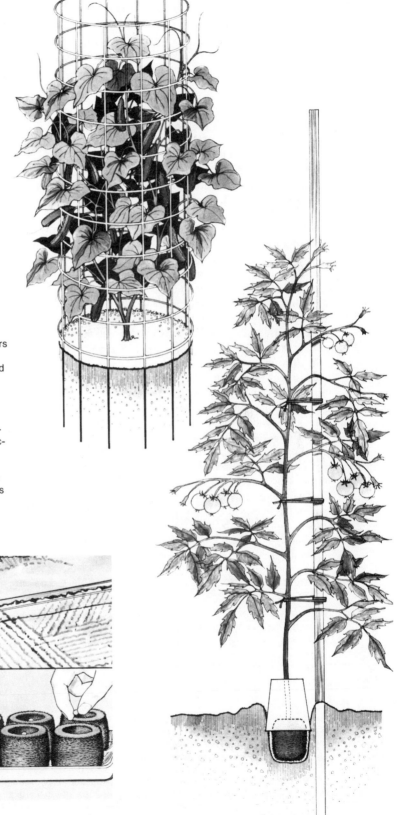

FENCING CAN be used to support cucumbers and melons, and let them climb (above). Tomatoes (right) should be staked when planted to avoid root injury later. Stakes up to seven feet high are recommended. Inverted paper cup at base of the plant will hold off hungry cutworms. Hoe handle (below) pressed into ground makes trench for planting seeds half-inch-deep. Cold frame (below, left) for protection and propagation of plants should be placed against a south wall or tight fence. Since frame usually is without bottom, drainage must be good. A good way to start seeds is in peat pellets (lower right). When sprouts are ready to be put out, you plant the entire pellet. Peat breaks down after it has been in the ground for a period of time.

Loose soil

Sandy soil is structurally the best for good root development, but if it is too sandy, it doesn't retain much moisture or nutrients. Solve the problem with compost or manure (again, one-third of the volume) along with peat moss. Since compost and manure break down to provide nourishment for plants, they should be replaced each year. Peat moss, while of no direct nutritive value, will remain in the soil for a long time, serving as a storehouse of water and fertilizer.

Acid or alkaline?

Soil pH is the measure of hydrogen ion concentration in the soil, which is, in turn, a measure of soil acidity. It can be determined to a fair degree of accuracy with a simple soil-test kit, available at a garden-supply store.

A pH reading of 1 is acid to the extreme, a pH 14 is as alkaline as you can get, and pH 7 is neutral soil. Most vegetables grow in slightly acid soil (pH 6 to 6.5). Much more acidity can be toxic to many plants, while very alkaline soil makes many trace elements unavailable to them.

The usual problem is acidity. If pH is below 5, add 10 pounds of ground limestone for each 100 square feet of garden. If it's only slightly low, make it 5 pounds. You can add it in the fall as a top dressing, giving you the chance to double check the reading in the spring, or put it on in the spring after having worked in the fertilizer. Rake it gently into the top inch of earth. Recheck the pH each year as lime is slowly leached out by rain.

If you live in an area rich in limestone, your soil problem is probably alkalinity. Fork in compost, manure, or peat moss to acidify. If the imbalance is extreme, say pH 8 or 9, add finely ground sulphur or aluminum sulfate.

Designing the plot

Maximum use of space is the keynote. Remember that space is three-dimensional, and that sun in the northern hemisphere comes from the south, particularly in early spring and late fall. This means that plants should be arranged

1. **WHEN SEEDLINGS** of root vegetables appear, thin out the weaker ones until there are but three or four plants to the inch. This allows remaining plants to grow to a good size. 2. Though the best defense against disease and pests is to maintain strong growth in plants, you may have to resort to sprays. There is a wide variety of chemical agents on the market. 3. A good "instant" mulch is provided by plastic covering. It holds in heat, discourages weeds. Plants grow through cutouts; slits provide ample drainage. 4. If you have planted crops in straight rows, cultivating with hoe is easy. A good time to weed is when the ground is moist from rain or soon after watering.

SPRING

In spring, seedlings must be "hardened off"—gradually acclimated to outside temperatures — before planting in ground. Crops shown here can be planted well before the last frost of spring, just about the time ground is workable. Care must be taken with cabbage. If a cold spell hits and plants are subjected to a week or more of daytime temperatures below 50°F., heads will begin to form prematurely

1 Spinach
2 Beets
3 Broccoli or cauliflower
4 Onions
5 Spinach
6 Early cabbage
7 Radishes
8 Early head lettuce
9 Peas

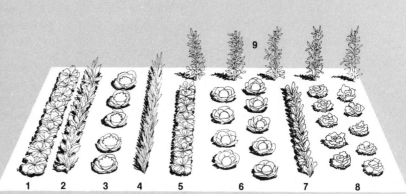

SUMMER

To give beans head start— and avoid possible frost injury—soak seeds indoors until almost germinated before planting in garden during a mild spell. Put in tomatoes, peppers and eggplant seedlings after all danger of frost is past. Follow in about a week with seed plantings of cucumbers, melons, pumpkins and squash.

1 Leaf lettuce
2 Carrots or parsley
3 Beets or kohlrabi
4 String beans
5 Onions (from spring planting harvest July)
6 Sweet pepper
7 Zucchini
8 Bush pumpkins
9 Eggplant
10 Tomatoes
11 Cucumbers

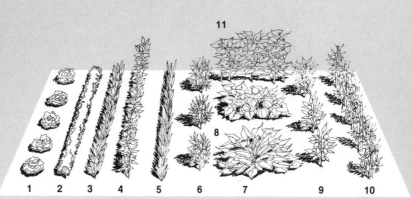

FALL

Lettuce, cabbage, beets, radishes, carrots, spinach and peas can all be planted in August or even September, depending on your area's climate. Again, planting seedlings will mean more of a harvest before winter. In all but the coldest climates, you can plant leaf lettuce, beets, carrots, onions and spinach in the fall and allow them to winter over for an exceedingly early harvest next spring. During the coldest of winter weather, you should cover crops with wood mulch.

Radishes
Parsley
Spinach
Radishes
5 Cabbage
6 Head lettuce seedlings
7 Peas

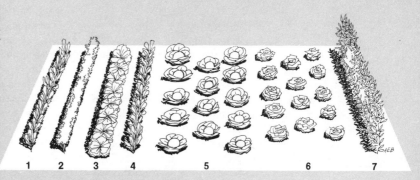

BEFORE FALL frost hits, cut off tomato vines at base and hang the plants upside-down to force ripening of the remaining fruit. You will find that onions will store well if they are hung in a dark, cool place.

not only as closely together as their well-being permits, but with the taller ones to the north so they won't shade the others.

Plant tomatoes in a line along the northern edge, about a foot apart and tied up on stakes or cattle fencing. Pinch off side shoots during early growth. Today's varieties are very fruitful, so it doesn't take many plants for a good crop.

Cucumbers and melons should also be allowed to climb, but no staking for them—they need cattle fencing or chicken wire. Cucumber vines easily support their fruit this way, but you may have to rig cloth slings to support cantaloupe and other melons as they get fully ripe.

Sweet peppers may need staking. The branches are quite brittle and crack easily under the weight of today's large peppers.

Harvest alternate plants

Plant cabbage and lettuce in twos or threes at close spacings. Head sizes won't be as large as they could be, but overall yield will be greater and be spread over a longer period. Harvest by pulling up an alternate plant every two or three days, as soon as the heads are developed enough to be edible. By the time you get back to the beginning of the row, the remaining plants should have nearly filled in the spaces. Don't let your lettuce harvest go into hot weather, as the heads will "bolt"—grow into stalks.

Beets, radishes, all the root vegetables, will benefit from the same alternating harvest principle, but practiced more extremely. Sprinkle seeds generously into a very straight, half-inch-deep trench—straightness will prove important when you're weeding the garden later—and let nature take its course. When the seedlings have appeared, thin out the weaker ones until you're left with three or four plants to the inch.

Allow plants to grow to a point where fruit formation is evident. Now thin out sparingly. Though fruit may not be large, it certainly will be edible. From then on, you'll be able to gather a small bunch of vegetables every week or two, taking them alternately from the row.

Onions are particularly good to grow in abundance. They can be stored by hanging them on a string in a dark, cool place, and will last all winter. You can buy onion "sets" (bulbs) at some garden shops for spring planting.

Starting seedlings

You can extend the productive life of much of your garden by starting seedlings in flats or pots. Tomatoes, eggplants and peppers will begin producing earlier and thus will last longer. Head lettuce will have time to head completely before the heat of summer causes bolting (growing into stalks). For the cabbage family, transplanted seedlings mean an earlier harvest.

Sow seeds near the surface in flats containing about two inches of loose, well-drained soil, six to eight weeks before you plan to put plants in the ground. Maintain a temperature of 70° to 75° F. until the seeds germinate. When the young sprouts have produced their first set of real leaves, they are ready to be transplanted to small pots, to other flats or to a cold frame. In frame or flat, allow two inches between plants.

Seedlings should be sprayed with Maneb to prevent "damping off"—a fungus that attacks the stems. Also, give the seedlings as much light as possible and guard against extreme humidity.

A simpler propagation method is to use peat pellets, sowing several seeds in each pellet and letting the strongest sprout remain. At the proper time, plant them in the ground, pellet and all. Easiest way is to buy seedlings ready for planting.

When to plant

The sample plot designs presented with this article allow for consecutive spring, summer and fall plantings, making the small garden as productive as possible. Harvest times of each season's plants roughly coincide with the times of planting of new crops.

The timetable reflects conditions of the lower New York State area, a moderate climate typical of much of continental U.S.A. Of course, growing seasons are shorter farther north and longer in the South. The fall planting schedule presented here applies only to areas where the first frost comes no earlier than the latter part of October or the fall season continues to be relatively mild even after a frost.

'Harden off' seedlings

Remember that all seedlings must be "hardened off"—they must have a week's exposure to gradually lower temperatures in making the transition from greenhouse warmth (or the sunny southern window where they've been kept) to outdoor temperatures.

Extra care should be taken with some crops. Cabbage, for example, should not go through a 7 to 10-day period of daytime temperatures consistently below 50° F. or heads will form prematurely.

Choosing varieties

Another result of the sophisticated hybrids developed is that there is a variety of every vegetable especially suited to nearly every specific locality. This is particularly true of tomatoes, eggplant, peppers and lettuce—in some cases a difference of 50 miles can call for two varieties. Most state agricultural colleges publish annual lists of recommended varieties by locality. These are available by mail. Your local agricultural agent will also have this information.

Diseases and pests

The best defense against disease and pests in the small garden is prevention. Maintain the plants in vigorous growth, remove all weeds from the plot and the close surroundings, and choose resistant strains of vegetables adapted to your region. To prevent cutworms from decapitating young seedlings, protect them with paper cups, the bottoms of which have been removed, when you put them in the ground.

Beyond this, weekly sprays or dustings of a pyrethrum-rotenone mixture can be very effective against a wide range of pests. Both substances are natural derivatives of plants and have a low toxicity to mammals. Caterpillars can be discouraged quite effectively with bacillus thuringiensis (sold under the trade names Dipel WP, Biotrol XK, and Thuricide HPC), which is nontoxic to mammals and other insects. This will prevent most of the damage done to members of the cabbage family.

Cabbages, brussels sprouts, cauliflower and kale also may suffer from maggots attacking their root stems. Onions and radishes may also be maggot victims. Use Malathion, a systemic spray that enters the plant's tissues. Malathion is also effective against leaf miners, a real problem in beets, turnips and leafy vegetables. These insects enter the leaf, leaving a telltale line of dead tissue to mark their paths as they eat it away. Malathion is one of the least toxic of the systemics, but that's not saying a lot.

Corn will almost certainly be attacked by many pests. Two of the worst, corn borer and earworm, can be prevented by applications of Sevin. This has a low toxicity to mammals, but is deadly to bees and many beneficial insects, so don't use it on anything in flower.

Fighting fungus diseases

Most fungus diseases can be controlled by selecting resistant strains of vegetables and maintaining the garden properly. In case of "club root," a fungus that greatly enlarges parts of the roots of cabbage, raising the pH of the soil to neutral is a good preventive.

Other likely fungus victims are the leaves of cucumbers and melons. Use Maneb, as directed, but only if you have to. Difolatan, Phaltan and Bravo are also very effective.

Probably the best preventive is also the simplest: Water in the morning rather than late in the day. Fungus likes it best when the soil is dark and damp at the same time.

Well, there you have it—a down-to-earth approach to the home vegetable garden. But before you begin, make sure there's room in the freezer for those late crops of beans, squash and other goodies. It is often surprising how many vegetables you end up with at the end of the season from a small garden plot.

Fruit and vegetable dryer you can build

INTERIOR VIEW shows how trays slide in and out. Two furnace filters at rear filter air from blower.

■ AN OLD AND satisfactory method of preserving food is by drying. This dryer uses a fan and two 300-watt heaters to maintain a temperature of about 120° F. and will dry a load in about 12 hours. Electrical consumption is low so the cost of drying a load is only about 25 cents.

To dry vegetables or fruit, you simply spread the food out in a single layer on screen-covered trays and then shift the trays from top to bottom during the drying period.

The dryer cabinet is made of ⅜-in. particle board and wood strips glued and nailed together. The front panel is held in place by two screw eyes that act as catches in the panel slots.

A small blower is attached to the underside of the cabinet to force air through the dryer. The two 300-w. heaters are mounted in the air outlet of the blower to heat the airstream. The cabinet is divided by two furnace filters.

The air safety switch, located at the blower

outlet, is actuated by the airflow and insures that the heaters will not operate unless the blower is providing air. The switch assembly is located after the blower and heater are installed. Bend the vane and locate the assembly so the airstream will raise the vane to actuate the switch. Be sure the switch opens when the vane falls. In the off position, the vane rests against the heaters. A thin sheet of aluminum is attached to the inside of the rear panel to reflect radiant heat.

Do not paint or finish the inside of the cabinet as this may taint the food.

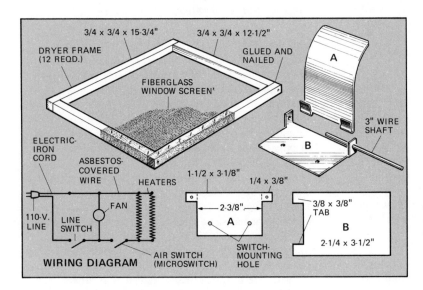

WIRING DIAGRAM

REAR VIEW, back removed, shows blower and heaters. Switch is in "on" position.

USE ⅜-in. particle board (not plywood) for drying compartment, and fiberglass window screen (not metal) to cover the food trays. Note air vent at top of door.

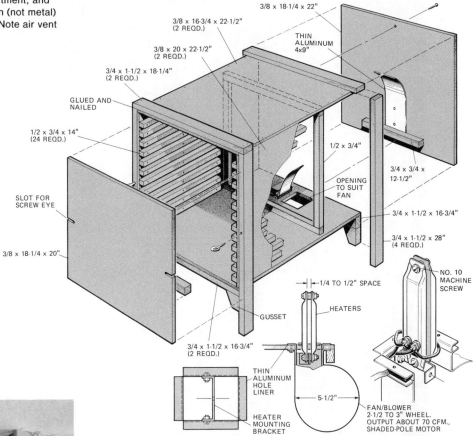

3/8 x 18-1/4 x 22"

3/8 x 16-3/4 x 22-1/2"
(2 REQD.)

THIN ALUMINUM 4x9"

3/8 x 20 x 22-1/2"
(2 REQD.)

3/4 x 1-1/2 x 18-1/4"
(2 REQD.)

GLUED AND NAILED

1/2 x 3/4 x 14"
(24 REQD.)

1/2 x 3/4"

OPENING TO SUIT FAN

3/4 x 3/4 x 12-1/2"

SLOT FOR SCREW EYE

3/4 x 1-1/2 x 16-3/4"

3/4 x 1-1/2 x 28"
(4 REQD.)

3/8 x 18-1/4 x 20"

GUSSET

3/4 x 1-1/2 x 16-3/4"
(2 REQD.)

1/4 TO 1/2" SPACE

HEATERS

NO. 10 MACHINE SCREW

THIN ALUMINUM HOLE LINER

HEATER MOUNTING BRACKET

5-1/2"

FAN/BLOWER 2-1/2 TO 3" WHEEL. OUTPUT ABOUT 70 CFM., SHADED-POLE MOTOR

BLOWER should have about 70-C.F.M. output. This one was from copier.

ACTUATING arm of air switch is bent to contact curved vane at hinge flap.

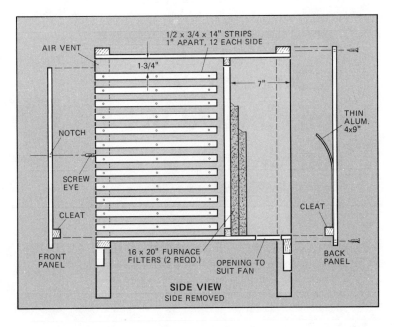

AIR VENT

1/2 x 3/4 x 14" STRIPS 1" APART, 12 EACH SIDE

1-3/4"

7"

NOTCH

SCREW EYE

THIN ALUM. 4x9"

CLEAT

CLEAT

FRONT PANEL

16 x 20" FURNACE FILTERS (2 REQD.)

OPENING TO SUIT FAN

BACK PANEL

SIDE VIEW
SIDE REMOVED

Greenhouse you can add to your home

YOU'LL HAVE a bumper crop of flowers blooming all year inside this beautiful greenhouse. The classic design will boost your house value.

■ THE SUN is shining, snow is on the ground, icicles are hanging from the roof, and the roses are blooming. This combination seems impossible, but there's one place it can happen—in a greenhouse, a beautiful addition to your home.

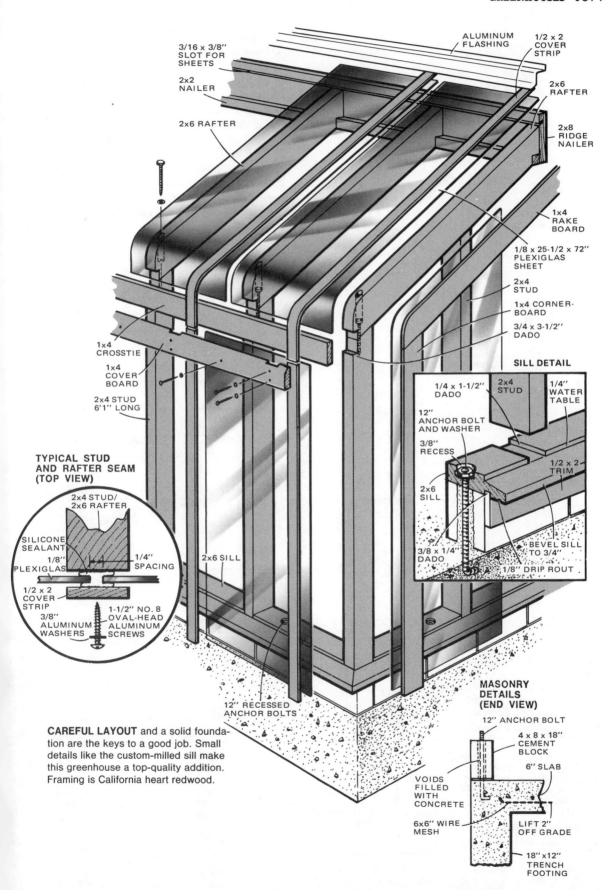

3/16 x 3/8"
SLOT FOR
SHEETS

2x2
NAILER

2x6 RAFTER

ALUMINUM
FLASHING

1/2 x 2
COVER
STRIP

2x6
RAFTER

2x8
RIDGE
NAILER

1x4
RAKE
BOARD

1/8 x 25-1/2 x 72"
PLEXIGLAS
SHEET

2x4
STUD

1x4 CORNER-
BOARD

3/4 x 3-1/2"
DADO

1x4
CROSSTIE

1x4
COVER
BOARD

2x4 STUD
6'1" LONG

**TYPICAL STUD
AND RAFTER SEAM
(TOP VIEW)**

2x4 STUD/
2x6 RAFTER

SILICONE
SEALANT

1/8"
PLEXIGLAS

1/4"
SPACING

1/2 x 2
COVER
STRIP

3/8"
ALUMINUM
WASHERS

1-1/2" NO. 8
OVAL-HEAD
ALUMINUM
SCREWS

2x6 SILL

SILL DETAIL

1/4 x 1-1/2"
DADO

2x4
STUD

1/4"
WATER
TABLE

12"
ANCHOR BOLT
AND WASHER

3/8"
RECESS

1/2 x 2
TRIM

2x6
SILL

3/8 x 1/4"
DADO

BEVEL SILL
TO 3/4"

1/8" DRIP ROUT

12" RECESSED
ANCHOR BOLTS

CAREFUL LAYOUT and a solid foundation are the keys to a good job. Small
details like the custom-milled sill make
this greenhouse a top-quality addition.
Framing is California heart redwood.

**MASONRY
DETAILS
(END VIEW)**

12" ANCHOR BOLT

4 x 8 x 18"
CEMENT
BLOCK

6" SLAB

VOIDS
FILLED
WITH
CONCRETE

6x6" WIRE
MESH

LIFT 2"
OFF GRADE

18" x 12"
TRENCH
FOOTING

The strong lean-to design of this greenhouse is so clean and simple that it will look good with any style home. You'll get the most use out of it in the winter when it captures enough of the sun's energy to keep your garden growing through the sleet and the snow. You can look forward to sitting "outside" in the greenhouse on a bright, 35 °F Sunday morning, and reading the papers in 75 °F comfort.

Making the greenhouse a part of your home gives you a lot of advantages. You'll need less material, and the adjacent house wall will protect the plants from winter winds. You'll be able to enter without going outside. You won't have to install lengthy electric or gas lines. But a great increase in heating efficiency is the best reason to go with a lean-to design. When there's no sun, you can let house heat spill into the greenhouse and take the load off its heater. When the sun is out, you can reverse this process and let that sweet hot-house air spill into the room and save on your fuel bill. It's the simplest form of solar heating.

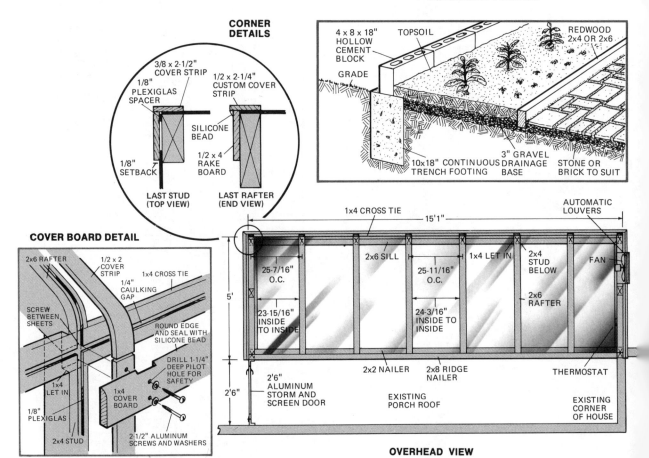

The structural design is simple, solid and flexible. Each bay is modular so you can add as many as you want to get just the right length. The height of the eaves is figured for a 6-ft. sheet of Plexiglas. This gives you comfortable headroom with the added height of the 8-in. cement block and sill. The run of the rafter also conforms to a 6-ft. sheet. We got extra space by attaching the ridge to an existing overhang. The design will also work against the flat wall of a house where you extend rafters and use 8-ft. sheets, another stock length.

Here's a rundown on the materials. The footings are concrete. We put down a full slab (a center drain is nice but unessential). You can also use a simpler and less costly perimeter footing (see alternate detail). The cement-block edging was laid while the concrete was still wet to get the best possible bond. This detail raises the wood sill off the ground and gives you more headroom. Many greenhouse designs call for a 3-ft. masonry wall; our design eliminates this expensive, time-consuming job and increases the growing area by letting in more light.

All timber is construction grade, heart redwood. It is milled from the center of the tree, contains virtually no sap, can be left untreated and still withstand high moisture. This is crucial since all sealers contain a mildecide agent with vapors that are harmful to plants months after application.

We chose ⅛-in. Plexiglas (even though it's softer than glass and more expensive than fiberglass) because it transmits light well, can be cut or trimmed easily (a sharp plywood blade will do it) and has an elegant appearance.

This is a large undertaking, but it's an addition with unusually high payoffs: good looks, a major jump in equity in your home, extra solar heat and, if you're an enterprising gardener, high-vitamin, unprocessed and nearly free vegetables.

Plexiglas comes slightly oversized, so we widened the framing centers and cut sheets down the middle. Be sure you comply with your local building codes. To maintain 60° F. on a cold day, your heater should produce 5000 B.T.U. for every 10 square feet of greenhouse.

One last note: Curving the Plexiglas to a wide arc is tricky with heat tape. Your supplier can bend the sheets to your design or you can use our alternate method for a single, tight bend at the eaves.

Greenhouse with cold frame extends the growing season

■ YOU CAN SOW the seeds for your vegetable garden early in the season inside this greenhouse. You can then harden the seedlings by moving them to the attached cold frame, before planting them outdoors when weather permits.

The combination structure allows you to start your planting season to ensure a good yield early—and throughout the planting season. The structure, built of readily available parts, can also be used to maintain flowering plants and lush foliage during the coldest winter months, when you'll be most grateful for the greenery.

A system of thermostatically controlled exhaust fans vents air from the greenhouse to the

FAN draws cool air in; stacked pair moves air from greenhouse to house.

DOUBLE ROOF vents draw off warm air from greenhouse by convection. Both are sealed in winter.

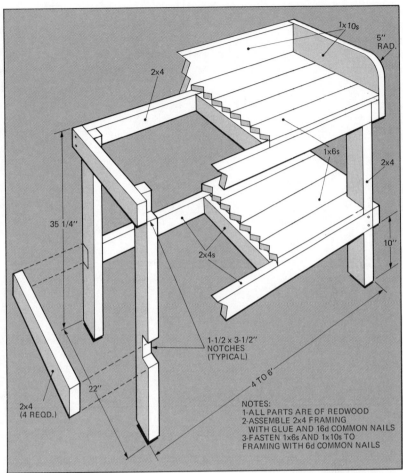

NOTES:
1-ALL PARTS ARE OF REDWOOD
2-ASSEMBLE 2x4 FRAMING
WITH GLUE AND 16d COMMON NAILS
3-FASTEN 1x6s AND 1x10s TO
FRAMING WITH 6d COMMON NAILS

house and outdoors. This provides the house with solar heat on sunny days and guards against the greenhouse overheating. These shutter-mounting exhaust fans are readily available.

For good heat retention, the greenhouse is glazed with 1-in.-thick double-glazed, patio-door replacement panels. Those on the roof are pitched at an angle to gain maximum solar benefits in the winter when the sun angle is low. The foundation is insulated with 2-in. Styrofoam as shown.

After determining the greenhouse location, lay out the exterior building lines using mason's line and pointed stakes; check corners for square. Determine the depth of the frostline for your area.

Excavate for the footings and foundation walls. You probably won't need forms to pour the footing. Simply dig a neat trench to required depth and width. The following foundation block wall is insulated, then covered by transite board.

The greenhouse floor consists of 6 in. of sand

covered with 2 in. of gravel. If you prefer, install a brick-in-sand floor covering. Just make certain that the 6-in. layer of sand is well compacted at the correct elevation. The sill is sealed and anchored to the cement blocks.

The greenhouse is framed with 2x6s, using conventional framing methods. Later, the framing members are clad with ¾-in. pine stock. Gussets are used on both sides of all sidewall roof joints.

Since the roof pitch may vary from that shown, complete all of the framing before measuring the two openings for the custom insulated glass. The eight other glass areas utilize standard patio-door replacement panes.

Install the ¾-in. pine jambs over the framing after the glass is in place and caulked. (In this design the interior jamb serves as the glass bead stops.) Important: Make certain the glass-wood joints are sealed, *inside and out*, with caulking.

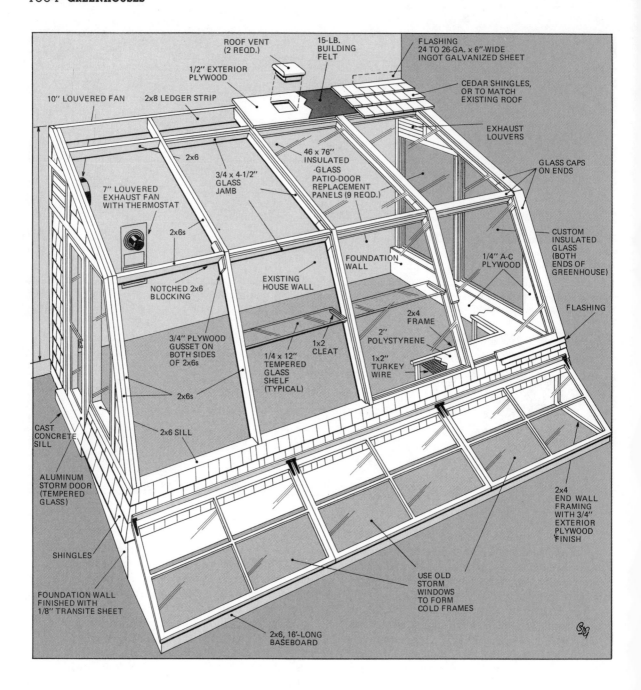

ROOF VENT (2 REQD.)

15-LB. BUILDING FELT

FLASHING 24 TO 26-GA. x 6"-WIDE INGOT GALVANIZED SHEET

1/2" EXTERIOR PLYWOOD

CEDAR SHINGLES, OR TO MATCH EXISTING ROOF

10" LOUVERED FAN

2x8 LEDGER STRIP

EXHAUST LOUVERS

2x6

46 x 76" INSULATED -GLASS PATIO-DOOR REPLACEMENT PANELS (9 REQD.)

GLASS CAPS ON ENDS

3/4 x 4-1/2" GLASS JAMB

7" LOUVERED EXHAUST FAN WITH THERMOSTAT

2x6s

CUSTOM INSULATED GLASS (BOTH ENDS OF GREENHOUSE)

FOUNDATION WALL

1/4" A-C PLYWOOD

NOTCHED 2x6 BLOCKING

EXISTING HOUSE WALL

FLASHING

2x4 FRAME

3/4" PLYWOOD GUSSET ON BOTH SIDES OF 2x6s

1/4 x 12" TEMPERED GLASS SHELF (TYPICAL)

1x2 CLEAT

2" POLYSTYRENE

1x2" TURKEY WIRE

2x6s

CAST CONCRETE SILL

2x6 SILL

ALUMINUM STORM DOOR (TEMPERED GLASS)

2x4 END WALL FRAMING WITH 3/4" EXTERIOR PLYWOOD FINISH

SHINGLES

USE OLD STORM WINDOWS TO FORM COLD FRAMES

FOUNDATION WALL FINISHED WITH 1/8" TRANSITE SHEET

2x6, 16'-LONG BASEBOARD

To make maximum use of the sunny space, you can install glass shelves as shown. Install a 1/4×12×46-in. tempered glass shelf across each of the six vertical glass areas. Each is supported by two 1×2 cleats 14 in. long.

The greenhouse also contains portable plant ledges propped on cement blocks. The ledges are framed with 2x4s to which 1x2-in. turkey wire has been fastened with 2-in. heavy-duty staples.

Two-in.-thick Styrofoam is placed over the frame to insulate transplanting flats.

The cold frame is constructed of 2x4 end walls sheathed with exterior plywood. A 2x6 board is installed between the end walls; used storm windows are hinged in place.

This sturdy redwood potting bench will give you an indoor work center for planting activities.

The work surface is a comfortable 35¼ in.

from the floor. However, you may want to shorten it to suit the user's height. Its legs are notched to receive the stretchers and rails, and it can be assembled with common nails. But ¼-in. carriage bolts, washers and nuts give a stronger bench.

Check the corners with a square before the glue dries. Wrack the unit square, if necessary, and tacknail diagonal strips from the legs to the top to hold it while the glue dries.

Before the glue dries, cut 1x6s to size for the shelf and benchtop. Attach with 6d common nails.

The splashboard is cut from 1x10 material. The sides and back are simply butt-joined at the corners. Round the ends on the sidepieces using a sabre or band saw; attach parts by 6d common nails and glue.

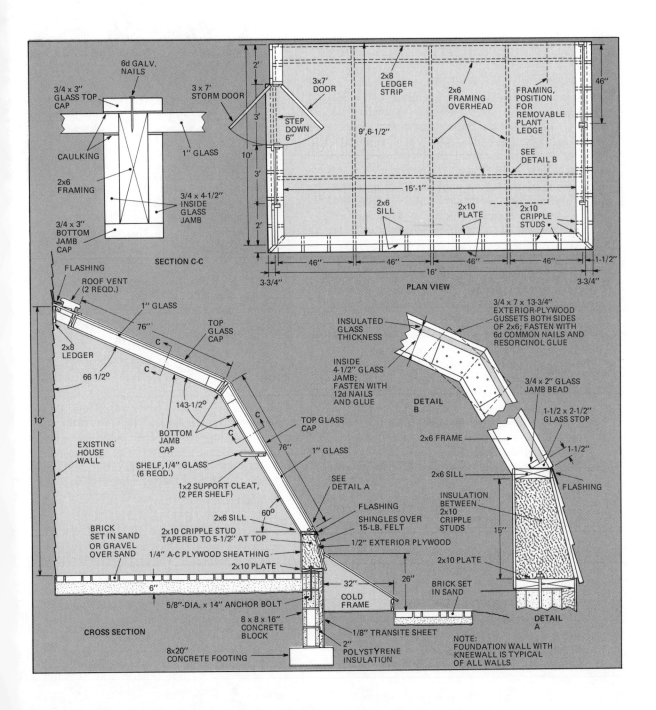

Greenhouse in your window

■ ADD A TOUCH of year-round beauty to your home by converting a window into a lush greenhouse. Decorative plants of different varieties will provide a display that can be enjoyed from the inside—and outside—of your home. If there's a gardener in the family, the window can double as a "hothouse" for propagating plants well in advance of the outdoor gardening season. Either way, certain features must be incorporated in order for the unit to be a true greenhouse.

• Provision for ventilating is necessary. Our version with operable top and bottom gives good air flow even with sash closed.

• If the climate and your growing plans dictate, you must have provisions for heating. On this model it's a simple matter to install a commercial electric heater.

• As in full-scale greenhouses, moisture must also be contained. Here, because window sash remains in place, you assure the greenhouse climate being independent of house climate.

• You must also be able to install supplementary plant lights if needed. On this model it is simply a matter of running in the electric wire.

• While a southern exposure is ideal because of its sun and warmth, other window locations can be used so long as they receive at least some direct sunlight during part of the day, especially in winter months.

Because the unit attaches with just four hooks and eyes, fastening in the window opening is easy. And the unit is self-contained; you don't have to remove the window sash. This means no drafts in the winter and no need for caulking or waterproofing.

Good construction features

Fashioned of ¼-in. Plexiglas and redwood, the box is designed so that the inside plane of the Plexiglas and frame are flush. As a result, all condensation collects on the bottom (which, in

turn, is pitched forward toward the front) on a water-impervious material where it can be removed by sliding back the bottom. Additionally, the bottom is easily removed for cleaning out any dirt or leaves that may collect.

To finish the greenhouse, apply two coats of exterior varnish to the redwood frame.

'Bubble' greenhouse

A plastic window garden fits inside a window like an air conditioner. The unit is ideal for those who are interested in getting the jump on spring by starting garden plants inside and moving them outdoors when weather permits. Instructions for mounting the bubble are packed in the carton. Installation time is about one hour. A tray for germinating seeds is included. If desired, it can be used instead to hold potted plants.

1. PLANT HANGERS are cut from ⅜-in. steel rods that, like all metal parts, are sprayed with flat black Rustoleum. **2.** Shelves of ¼-in. Plexiglas are cut to length and 12 in. wide. When a 1½-in. flange is bent along each side a shelf width of 9 in. is left. **3.** The unit shown is held in position with four screw eyes and hooks. Foam tape keeps out any drafts and water from entering. **4.** The plastic top is held in open position with one wood hinge at each end. A spring prevents the top from chattering in stiff breezes.

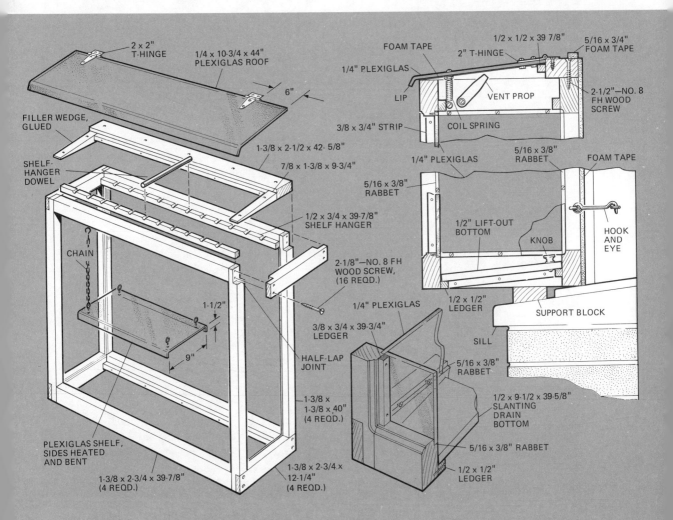

2 × 2" T-HINGE

1/4 × 10-3/4 × 44" PLEXIGLAS ROOF

6"

FILLER WEDGE, GLUED

SHELF-HANGER DOWEL

1-3/8 × 2-1/2 × 42-5/8"

7/8 × 1-3/8 × 9-3/4"

1/2 × 3/4 × 39-7/8" SHELF HANGER

CHAIN

2-1/8"—NO. 8 FH WOOD SCREW, (16 REQD.)

3/8 × 3/4 × 39-3/4" LEDGER

1-1/2"

9"

HALF-LAP JOINT

1-3/8 × 1-3/8 × 40" (4 REQD.)

PLEXIGLAS SHELF, SIDES HEATED AND BENT

1-3/8 × 2-3/4 × 39-7/8" (4 REQD.)

1-3/8 × 2-3/4 × 12-1/4" (4 REQD.)

FOAM TAPE

2" T-HINGE

1/4" PLEXIGLAS

LIP

1/2 × 1/2 × 39 7/8"

5/16 × 3/4" FOAM TAPE

VENT PROP

2-1/2"—NO. 8 FH WOOD SCREW

3/8 × 3/4" STRIP

COIL SPRING

1/4" PLEXIGLAS

5/16 × 3/8" RABBET

5/16 × 3/8" RABBET

FOAM TAPE

1/2" LIFT-OUT BOTTOM

KNOB

HOOK AND EYE

1/2 × 1/2" LEDGER

SUPPORT BLOCK

SILL

1/4" PLEXIGLAS

5/16 × 3/8" RABBET

1/2 × 9-1/2 × 39-5/8" SLANTING DRAIN BOTTOM

5/16 × 3/8" RABBET

1/2 × 1/2" LEDGER

Portable electric grill you can build

■ WHEN YOUR GUESTS are having a ball and you're slaving over a hot stove in the kitchen, entertaining friends is not all fun. With this electric grill-on-wheels the host can join the fun from the start and charbroil mouth-watering

steaks right in the center of the party.

You install the drop-in grill in a smart roll-about cabinet (which we show you how to build) rather than in a kitchen counter so you can be with your friends right where the action is.

To enjoy this modern indoor cooking, you roll the cabinet up to a "porthole" in an outside wall, connect the grill to it with a 24-in. flexible duct and plug the cord into a 240-v. outlet. In seconds you have 2800 watts of clean radiant heat which will charbroil steaks, hamburgers, hot dogs, fish or fowl faster than an outdoor grill. A powerful below-the-surface fan pulls smoke and fumes directly into the exhaust system without a trace in the room.

There are several gourmet accessories you can add, including a rotisserie, shish kebab skewers

and french fryer. A kit of parts for wiring and ducting the grill outdoors is also available.

When the grill is not in use, snug-fitting caps plug the exhaust ports in both the wall and cabinet. The duct and cable store inside and the cabinet top folds shut to hide the grill.

The boxlike design of the handsome Danish-modern cabinet helps simplify construction. It's **made entirely of oak-veneer plywood, stained dark brown except for the black-painted base and the bottom shelf.** Butt joints are used for the most part and reinforced on the inside with square blocks glued in the corners. Both ends are the same size, but right- and left-hand, with a 5-in.-dia. hole being cut in the right-hand one. Both are blind-grooved on the inside at the front for the bottom crossrail. The back butts between the ends, as do the grill cutout, the 3⅜-in. crossrail and the bottom. The storage section of the cabinet is fitted with twin doors and equipped with suitable pulls and magnetic catches. There's a lot of storage room here for all of your cooking and party needs.

The two-piece top is joined with piano hinges and supported when open by handles on the ends of the cabinet. Flip-down aprons hinged to the grill cutout, front and back, support the top when closed; spring-loaded friction catches placed at the ends of the aprons hold them in an upright position.

The electric grill sits in the hole provided and is secured in place with locking screws. Two standard 5-in. elbows and a straight section of galvanized smoke pipe are needed to duct the

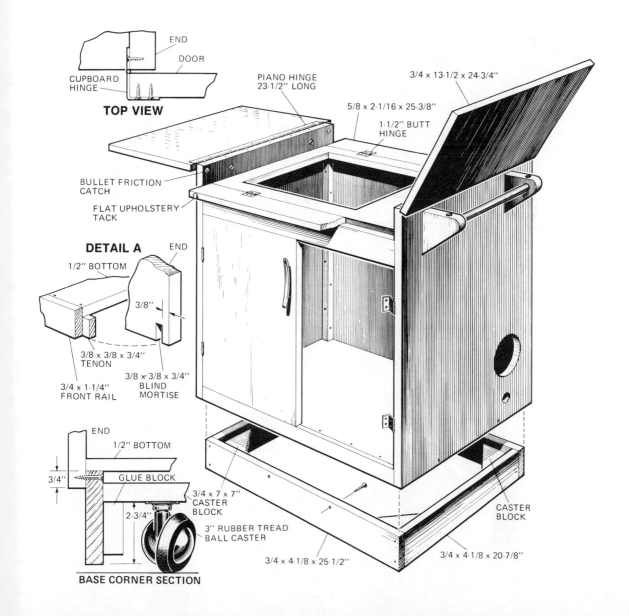

TOP VIEW

END
DOOR
CUPBOARD HINGE

PIANO HINGE 23-1/2'' LONG

3/4 x 13-1/2 x 24-3/4''

5/8 x 2-1/16 x 25-3/8''

1-1/2'' BUTT HINGE

BULLET FRICTION CATCH

FLAT UPHOLSTERY TACK

DETAIL A
END
1/2'' BOTTOM
3/8''
3/8 x 3/8 x 3/4'' TENON
3/8 x 3/8 x 3/4'' BLIND MORTISE
3/4 x 1-1/4'' FRONT RAIL

END
1/2'' BOTTOM
3/4''
GLUE BLOCK
2-3/4''
3/4 x 7 x 7'' CASTER BLOCK
3'' RUBBER TREAD BALL CASTER
3/4 x 4-1/8 x 25-1/2''
3/4 x 4-1/8 x 20-7/8''
CASTER BLOCK

BASE CORNER SECTION

SNUG-FITTING CAP (above) plugs duct hole in cabinet when the grill is not used. Interior view (right) shows how the grill blower is piped outside with two 5-in.-dia. galvanized furnace pipe elbows fastened together.

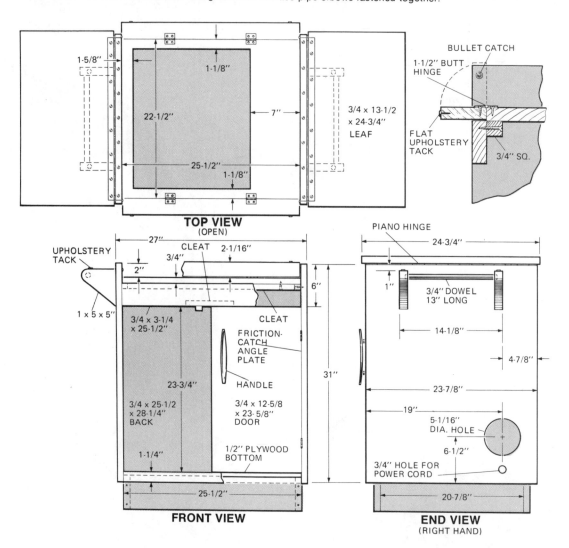

1-5/8"

1-1/8"

22-1/2"

7"

3/4 x 13-1/2
x 24-3/4"
LEAF

25-1/2"

1-1/8"

TOP VIEW
(OPEN)

BULLET CATCH

1-1/2" BUTT
HINGE

FLAT
UPHOLSTERY
TACK

3/4" SQ.

UPHOLSTERY
TACK

1 x 5 x 5"

27"

CLEAT

2-1/16"

3/4"

2"

6"

3/4 x 3-1/4
x 25-1/2"

CLEAT

FRICTION-
CATCH
ANGLE
PLATE

HANDLE

23-3/4"

31"

3/4 x 25-1/2
x 28-1/4"
BACK

3/4 x 12-5/8
x 23-5/8"
DOOR

1/2" PLYWOOD
BOTTOM

1-1/4"

25-1/2"

FRONT VIEW

PIANO HINGE

24-3/4"

1"

3/4" DOWEL
13" LONG

14-1/8"

4-7/8"

23-7/8"

19"

5-1/16"
DIA. HOLE

6-1/2"

3/4" HOLE FOR
POWER CORD

20-7/8"

END VIEW
(RIGHT HAND)

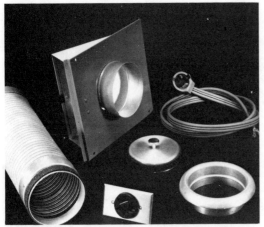

KIT OF PARTS includes two rings, two caps, flexible duct, damper, power cord and a 240-v. receptacle.

DUCT THROUGH house wall (above, left) is capped outside with butterfly damper attached with screws.

ventilating fan through the hole in the side of the cabinet. An aluminum ring that comes with the kit fits the hole on the outside. The outdoor exhaust port is installed by cutting a 5-in. hole through the wall and inserting a 5-in. section of 5-in. galvanized pipe. The pipe is then fitted with a ring on the inside and a damper on the outside. Since the unit is on ball casters it can be rolled from room to room, and additional outdoor exhaust ports can be placed in the kitchen or wherever you want to cook.

EXHAUST PORT in outside wall is located 12 in. from floor. The 240-v. receptacle is shown adjacent.

HANDY CONDIMENT rack is attached to left-hand door. Details (below) show how the rack is assembled.

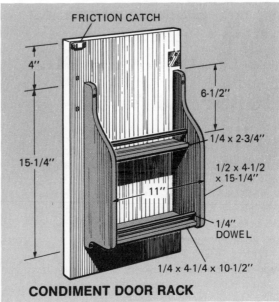

FRICTION CATCH

4"

6-1/2"

1/4 x 2-3/4"

15-1/4"

1/2 x 4-1/2 x 15-1/4"

11"

1/4" DOWEL

1/4 x 4-1/4 x 10-1/2"

CONDIMENT DOOR RACK

NOTHING RUSTS FASTER than a portable grill and cooking utensils that are left exposed to the weather. This good-looking shelter provides protection and a handy work surface.

Weatherproof house for your grill

■ OUTDOOR COOKING can be more work than pleasure if it means you have to round up the necessary gear each time—from the kitchen and a cluttered garage or basement.

With a weatherproof shelter for your grill, supplies and utensils, cookouts will be a lot less trouble. This shelter has a slide-out workshelf and room enough to keep everything handy.

Before building, choose the unit's location carefully, making sure drainage is good. Since the structure may be considered a permanent addition to your property, check local codes to determine whether a building permit will be required. You may wish to attach the unit to your house or to a fence or privacy screen. If so, change the dimensions to suit; if it will butt against the house, it must be properly flashed to prevent leaks.

Begin construction by setting a floor of patio blocks in concrete, with anchor bolts protruding through holes drilled in four of the blocks. (This slab should rest on footings.) Framing is with 2x4s. Start the framing with one middle section and two end sections. Since the middle and one end are identical, one frame can serve as a pattern for the other. Horizontal members tie the sections together into a boxlike frame.

Both roof and slide-out shelf are made from a ¼-in. aluminum-clad plywood product available at lumberyards. Above the slide-out shelf is a wider storage shelf, which may be easier to install if sawed in half and rejoined in place. Fixed shelves are notched to fit framing. When shelves have been installed, the roof can be added and trimmed with 1×3s. Then ½ × 3½-in. tongue-and-groove western cedar siding is applied vertically and blindnailed to the 2×4 cross members for a weathertight wall. Doors are made of the same siding, blindnailed to 1×4 diagonal bracing using a jig of cleats nailed to your workbench or a sheet of plywood.

Use 10d common nails to spike the 2x4s together and 8d common nails to toenail them. Sid-

THE SHELTER keeps cooking equipment and supplies together. Shelf provides a work surface.

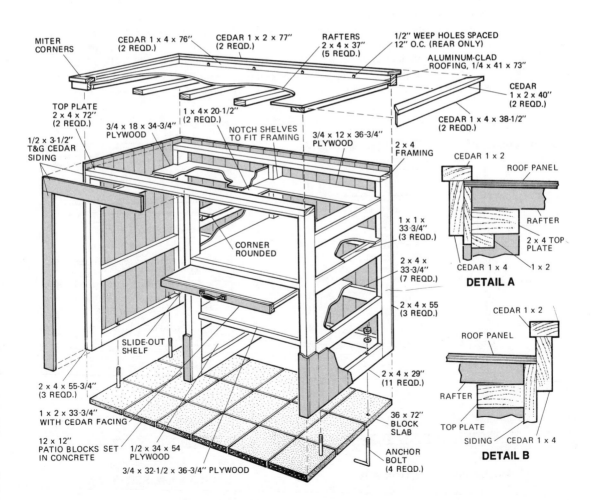

MITER CORNERS

CEDAR 1 x 4 x 76"
(2 REQD.)

CEDAR 1 x 2 x 77"
(2 REQD.)

RAFTERS
2 x 4 x 37"
(5 REQD.)

1/2" WEEP HOLES SPACED
12" O.C. (REAR ONLY)

ALUMINUM-CLAD
ROOFING, 1/4 x 41 x 73"

CEDAR
1 x 2 x 40"
(2 REQD.)

CEDAR 1 x 4 x 38-1/2"
(2 REQD.)

TOP PLATE
2 x 4 x 72"
(2 REQD.)

3/4 x 18 x 34-3/4"
PLYWOOD

1 x 4 x 20-1/2"
(2 REQD.)

NOTCH SHELVES
TO FIT FRAMING

3/4 x 12 x 36-3/4"
PLYWOOD

2 x 4
FRAMING

1/2 x 3-1/2"
T&G CEDAR
SIDING

CORNER
ROUNDED

1 x 1 x
33-3/4"
(3 REQD.)

2 x 4 x
33-3/4"
(7 REQD.)

2 x 4 x 55
(3 REQD.)

SLIDE-OUT
SHELF

2 x 4 x 29"
(11 REQD.)

2 x 4 x 55-3/4"
(3 REQD.)

1 x 2 x 33-3/4"
WITH CEDAR FACING

36 x 72"
BLOCK
SLAB

12 x 12"
PATIO BLOCKS SET
IN CONCRETE

1/2 x 34 x 54
PLYWOOD

ANCHOR
BOLT
(4 REQD.)

3/4 x 32-1/2 x 36-3/4" PLYWOOD

CEDAR 1 x 2

ROOF PANEL

RAFTER

2 x 4 TOP
PLATE

CEDAR 1 x 4

1 x 2

DETAIL A

CEDAR 1 x 2

ROOF PANEL

RAFTER

TOP PLATE

SIDING

CEDAR 1 x 4

DETAIL B

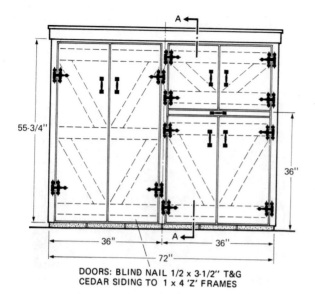

55-3/4"

36"

36"   36"

72"

DOORS: BLIND NAIL 1/2 x 3-1/2" T&G
CEDAR SIDING TO 1 x 4 'Z' FRAMES

THE CLOSED SHELTER gives weathertight protection
of its contents. The roof slopes ¾ in. to the back
and drains through weep holes in the rear fascia

ing and ¾-in. lumber require 6d finishing nails.
The roof is attached to the rafters with neoprene
washer roofing nails 12 in. apart, then caulked.
Friction catches hold the doors closed.

The structure can be stained or painted after
doors are hung; use saw-textured siding with stain.
Wood siding other than cedar may be used, and
other styles of siding are also possible. For best
appearance, use the same material for both walls

and fascia. Since the unit shown butts against
house siding, its corner pieces were notched to fit.

The shelter is designed so that it can be readily
adapted to other uses, such as for storage of
garden tools or outdoor sports equipment. Pool-
side use is another possibility. The unit could also
include a weatherproof electrical outlet, allowing
temporary installation of a portable refrigerator in
the lower cabinet for entertaining.

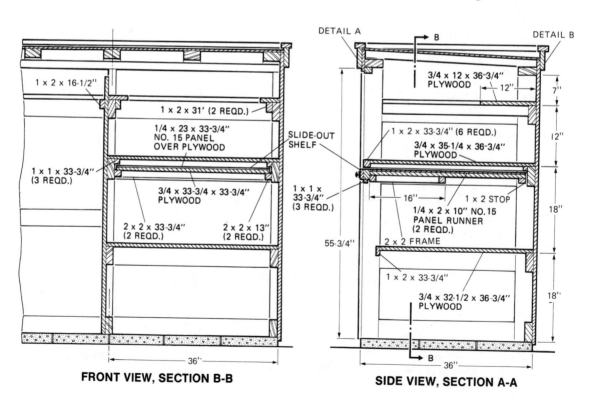

1 x 2 x 16-1/2"

1 x 2 x 31' (2 REQD.)

1/4 23 x 33-3/4"
NO. 15 PANEL
OVER PLYWOOD

1 x 1 x 33-3/4"
(3 REQD.)

3/4 x 33-3/4 x 33-3/4"
PLYWOOD

2 x 2 x 33-3/4"
(2 REQD.)

2 x 2 x 13"
(2 REQD.)

36"

FRONT VIEW, SECTION B-B

DETAIL A   B   DETAIL B

3/4 x 12 x 36-3/4"
PLYWOOD   12"   7"

SLIDE-OUT
SHELF

1 x 1 x
33-3/4"
(3 REQD.)

1 x 2 x 33-3/4" (6 REQD.)
3/4 x 35-1/4 x 36-3/4"
PLYWOOD   12"

1 x 2 STOP

16"

1/4 x 2 x 10" NO.15
PANEL RUNNER
(2 REQD.)   18"

2 x 2 FRAME

55-3/4"

1 x 2 x 33-3/4"

3/4 x 32-1/2 x 36-3/4"
PLYWOOD   18"

B

36"

SIDE VIEW, SECTION A-A

BASED ON standard shelf hardware system, this rack puts your present gun collection on display, with flexibility and room for future acquisitions. Guns are supported at both ends by blocks that are fastened to the cut-down shelf brackets.

Gun rack that's custom-fit

■ PUTTING INOPERATIVE GUNS on display is quick work with a rack that makes use of shelf hardware for fast construction and flexibility. Each gun is fitted to its own brackets, assuring solid support and level display for best appearance. Guns can be repositioned and respaced easily and standards can also support a shelf, as shown above, for accessories.

The shelf system used here has satin-finish brass brackets, custom cut with a hacksaw blade. Support blocks were cut from ¾-in. pine and stained walnut. Scraps of an attractive hardwood such as walnut or birch could also be used. Blocks, used as templates for laying out cuts to be made on brackets, are shaped first to fit guns on a cut-and-try basis or, better, cut to cardboard templates fitted to gun contours. Rear (stock) supports are made first; then each gun is held in position and heights and depths of front (barrel) supports are figured so guns will be level.

BRASS SHELF brackets are surprisingly easy to cut with hacksaw blade in sabre saw. Wood block is first cut to fit gun, then temporarily attached to bracket as template for marking cuts. Final assembly is with ¾-in. No. 8 flathead brass woodscrews. Use a countersink made for metal on the brackets. Note: a locking cabinet and trigger locks should be used for display of operable weapons.

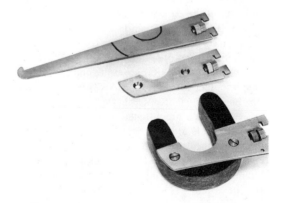

Oil-proof gun rack

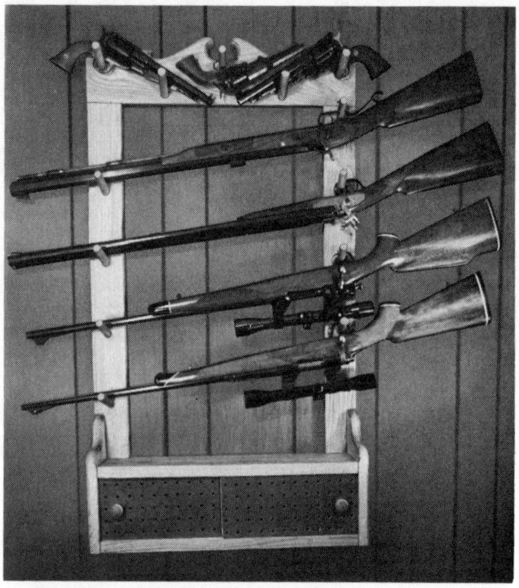

■ THIS GUN RACK holds guns upside down with their muzzles at the low point. This prevents oil from saturating and weakening the wood stock. The rack holds long guns and handguns by their trigger guards. The firearms hang on dowel pegs, which aren't likely to dent or scratch the stocks. If there are children in the house, store ammunition elsewhere and use trigger or cable locks.

Cut out a cardboard pattern using a 1-in. grid before you cut the top of the rack (part A). Then outline the pattern on the wood, bore out waste in the four circular curves with a ¾-in.-dia. bit and cut out the part on a band saw.

Join the rack sides and top with glue and screws in corner lap joints. Use a try square to lay out the parts and draw lines for the width of the lap cuts. Then use a table saw to make a ⅜-in.-deep shoulder cut; turn the stock on edge, set the rip fence and clear out the waste. The vertical legs of the rack are notched and rabbeted to receive the ends and bottom of the compartment. Mark the locations and bore ¾-in.-dia. x ⅝-in. deep holes at an angle for the rack pegs.

The compartment top, bottom, back and ends are cut of pine. The doors for the compartment are of perforated hardboard and they slide in grooves cut in the compartment top and bottom pieces. The top is notched to fit around the rack legs. The compartment's top fits into blind dadoes in the end pieces.

Test-fit the compartment parts, then sand them smooth with 120-grit abrasive, tack off and attach knobs to the doors before joining parts with carpenter's glue. Apply stain and finish as desired.

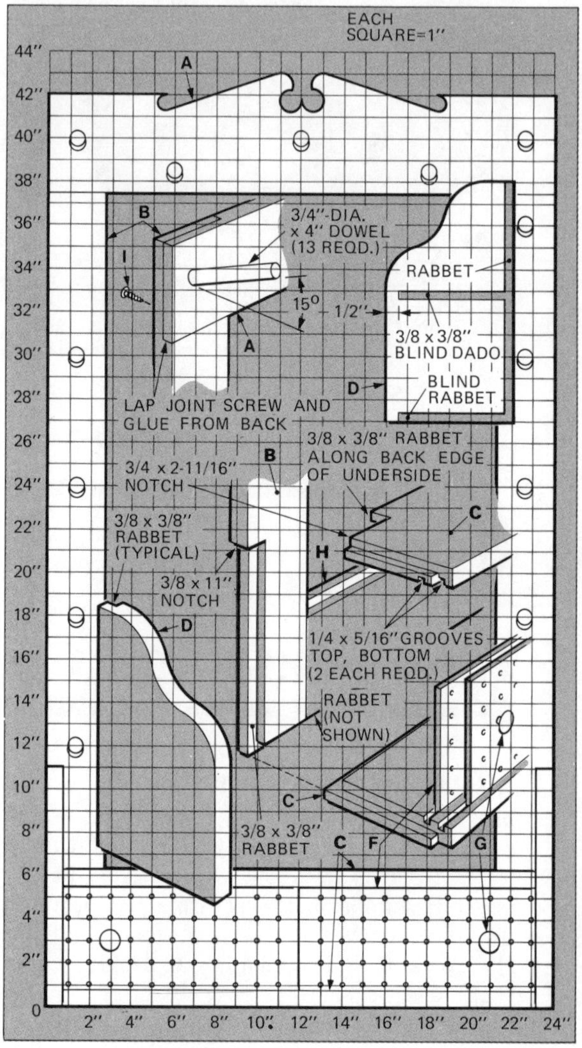

MATERIALS LIST—GUN RACK

Key	No.	Size and Description (use)
A	1	¾ x 5½ x 24" pine (rack top)
B	2	¾ x 2$^{11}/_{16}$ x 41⅝" pine (vertical members; rip a 1 x 6 in half)
C	2	¾ x 5½ x 23¼" pine (compartment top, bottom)
D	2	¾ x 5½ x 11" pine (compartment ends)
E	13	¾"-dia. x 4" dowel (rack pegs)
F	2	¼ x 5¼ x 12" perforated hardboard (doors)
G	2	1"-dia. wooden knobs
H	1	¾ x 5½ x 18⅝" pine (compartment back)
I	*	⅜" No. 10 fh wood screws

Misc.: Carpenter's glue; stain and finish. *As required.

Cabinet for your guns

■ THIS CABINET consists of two separate assemblies, a top and a bottom. We used solid stock throughout in building it, although hardwood-faced plywood would be adequate for the side panels of each assembly.

Start the top assembly first by cutting the sides to size and rabbeting the top and back edges. The top board is cut ¼ in. narrower than the

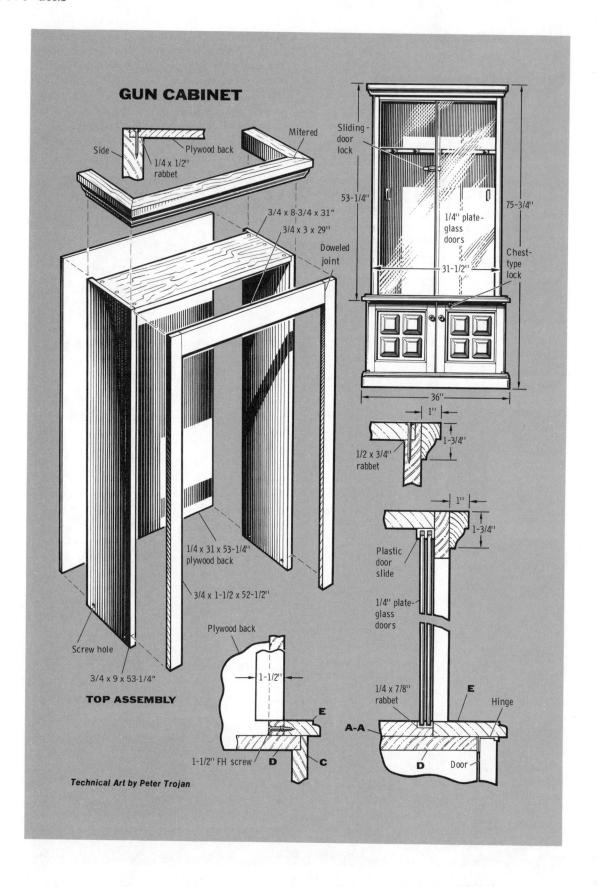

GUN CABINET

Side

Plywood back

1/4 x 1/2" rabbet

Mitered

3/4 x 8-3/4 x 31"

3/4 x 3 x 29"

Doweled joint

1/4 x 31 x 53-1/4" plywood back

3/4 x 1-1/2 x 52-1/2"

Screw hole

3/4 x 9 x 53-1/4"

TOP ASSEMBLY

Plywood back

1-1/2"

E

1-1/2" FH screw   D   C

Sliding-door lock

53-1/4"

1/4" plate-glass doors

31-1/2"

75-3/4"

Chest-type lock

36"

1"

1-3/4"

1/2 x 3/4" rabbet

1"

1-3/4"

Plastic door slide

1/4" plate-glass doors

1/4 x 7/8" rabbet

E

A-A

Hinge

D   Door

Technical Art by Peter Trojan

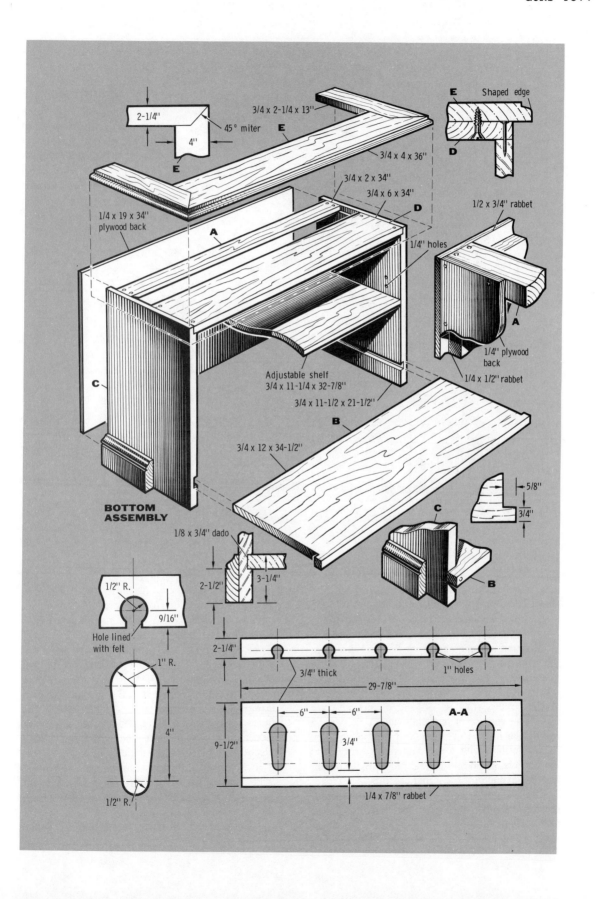

2-1/4"

45° miter

4"

E

3/4 x 2-1/4 x 13"

E

3/4 x 4 x 36"

E   Shaped edge

D

3/4 x 2 x 34"

3/4 x 6 x 34"

D

1/2 x 3/4" rabbet

1/4 x 19 x 34"
plywood back

A

1/4" holes

A

1/4" plywood
back

1/4 x 1/2" rabbet

C

Adjustable shelf
3/4 x 11-1/4 x 32-7/8"

3/4 x 11-1/2 x 21-1/2"

B

3/4 x 12 x 34-1/2"

BOTTOM
ASSEMBLY

C

5/8"

3/4"

B

1/8 x 3/4" dado

1/2" R.

9/16"

Hole lined
with felt

2-1/2"

3-1/4"

1" R.

4"

1/2" R.

2-1/4"

3/4" thick

1" holes

29-7/8"

9-1/2"

6"   6"

3/4"

A-A

1/4 x 7/8" rabbet

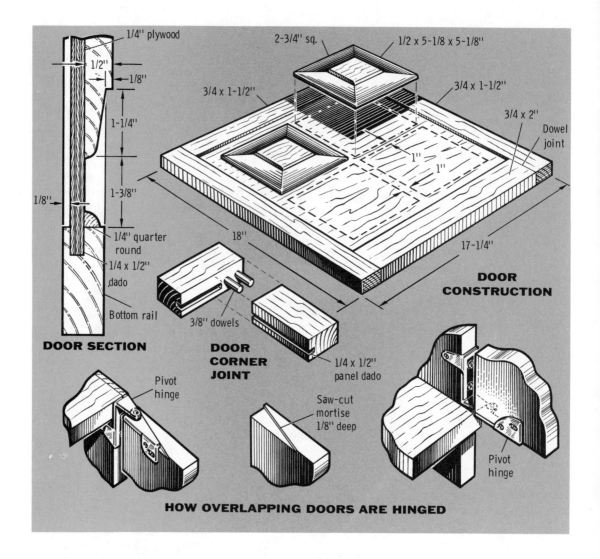

1/4'' plywood

1/2''

1/8''

1-1/4''

1-3/8''

1/8''

1/4'' quarter round

1/4 x 1/2'' dado

Bottom rail

DOOR SECTION

2-3/4'' sq.

1/2 x 5-1/8 x 5-1/8''

3/4 x 1-1/2''

3/4 x 1-1/2''

3/4 x 2''

Dowel joint

1''

1''

18''

17-1/4''

DOOR CONSTRUCTION

3/8'' dowels

1/4 x 1/2'' panel dado

DOOR CORNER JOINT

Pivot hinge

Saw-cut mortise 1/8'' deep

Pivot hinge

HOW OVERLAPPING DOORS ARE HINGED

side members to accommodate the ¼-in. plywood back, and the back member is cut ¾ in. longer than the sides so it can be fastened to the bottom assembly.

Glue and nail the parts together and then face the front edges with a three-piece frame. This is made the same width as the assembled unit (31½ in.) but is cut ¾ in. shorter. It's doweled at the corners, then glued and clamped to the unit. You can use a few nails across the top in pre-drilled holes since they will be hidden. The top is finished with a molding that's mitered at the corners, glued and brought flush with the top board. So much for the upper assembly.

The bottom assembly is built similarly in that the top and rear edges of the sides are rabbeted as before. In addition, a ⅛ x ¾-in. dado is made in each side member for a bottom shelf. The lat-

ter is notched at the front corners so it will project ¾ in. across the front. Facing rows of ¼-in. blind holes (fitted with shelf brackets) hold the adjustable center shelf.

After the parts are glued and nailed together, a ¾ x 3¼-in. base molding is mitered and glued around the bottom. Finally, the three pieces which make up the top sill (E), are mitered and doweled, then shaped with a router along the outer edge. The sill is attached to the base with glue and screws, the latter being driven through pieces A and D from the underside.

The top assembly is attached to the bottom with four screws driven through the side members from the inside. Nails can be used to fasten the plywood across the back.

Part A-A slips in place behind part E. While in each case it's rabbeted across the front for a plastic door slide, you can forget about cutting the gunstock pits in it if you plan to use the cabinet as a bookcase or china cabinet.

The stock pits are cut completely through the board, then backed up on the bottom. The neatest way to cut the pits is to bore holes at each end of the cutout and then saw out the waste. If you have a router, you can do the job quickly with a jig you make to guide the machine. Pieces of felt are later cut and glued to line the bottom of the pits. Part A-A is left loose, and the space between pieces A and D permits piece A-A to be pushed out to give future access to the four screws which hold the top section.

This leaves the doors. Each consists of a ¼-in. plywood panel framed on four sides with grooved members. Four square overlays cut from ½-in. solid stock are glued to the center panel. These are beveled by tilting the blade on your table saw and running the work on edge. A sandpaper block is used to round off the outer edges.

The details show how the doors are attached at the top and bottom with pivoting pin hinges.

The notches in the barrel rack are made with a 1-in. drill and then sawed through. The size of the notches and the location of the rack in the case are governed by the size of your guns.

If the cabinet is to be used for guns, both glass and wood doors should be fitted with locks. If one of the wood doors is fitted with an overlapping metal stop, one lock will lock both doors. The lock you'll need for the glass doors is a showcase lock, whereas a regular chest lock will do for the wooden doors. Here it is wise to have the latter on hand before adding the sill piece E to the base since it will require cutting a mortise on the underside of the piece to receive the latch. Routing the mortise will be a lot easier to do before E is glued and screwed in place.

The two plate-glass doors measure 15 x 51½". These you'll have to have cut, with edges rounded and finger grips ground in the surface. They slide in plastic tracks placed at top and bottom.

The best old guns are new

■ GOOD REPLICA GUNS and modern muzzleloaders are not cheap. But compared with collector originals, they are bargains indeed. What's more, replicas do a better job of demonstrating how the originals handled, and for that matter, how they shot, than the classics could do themselves today.

How can that be? Easy. Most of the original Revolutionary arms are in museums or private collections and are too valuable to risk firing. Those in good shape are too good to be used and the bad ones are either nonworking, unsafe, or both. A good modern replica, however, feels like an original, fires like an original, and can give the real sensation of what old-time shooting was like.

An original Whitworth military target rifle, for example, of the type used by some Confederate snipers and English target shooters, might cost $2,000 to $4,000 in good condition today. The Navy Arms replica of the Whitworth is gauged by the same gauges that were used to inspect the originals in the 1860s. The new barrels have the identical hexagonal rifling making one turn in 20 inches that enabled the original Whitworth to hit a 30-inch target at up to 1000 yards. The replicas not only look the same, they shoot as well or better using modern cast lead bullets. Matches for these and other slug guns—so-called because they shoot a conical bullet or slug rather than the round ball of many other muzzleloading rifles—are featured in numerous black powder matches.

DIXIE GUN WORKS' modern muzzleloader (left) is Tennessee flintlock squirrel rifle. Customized Kentucky flint long rifle, by George Heinemann, replicates 1790 styling. Whitworth hexagonal-bore sniper rifle (center), from Navy Arms, has 1,000-yard range. Percussion Hawken II by Navy Arms is suitable field rifle for deer hunting. Navy Magnum 12-gauge shotgun (right) is a black powder choice for clay pigeons and waterfowl. Flintlock pistol copies specifications for British Army 1761 Dragoon.

CASED dueling pistols would cost thousands for the 1870 originals.

FAVORITE OLD hideaways for pistols were imitation books.

1750 TINDERLIGHTER is a neat way to strike light for the attached candle.

ETHAN ALLEN model (top) is a pepperbox. Mountain Pistol. Ruger Old Army revolver is available in stainless steel. Lincoln derringer (bottom) comes either factory-finished or as kit.

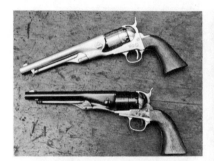

THOMPSON CENTER Cougar Hawken (top) and reissued Colt 1860 Army are in stainless steel.

COLT'S REISSUED 1860 Army .44 is of stainless steel.

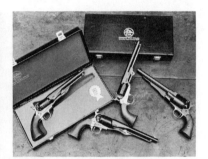

FROM CVA are (left to right) 1861 Colt Navy, 1860 Colt Army, 1851 brass-frame Navy and 1858 Remington .44.

Since 1954, when the first mass-produced muzzleloading rifle and pistol replicas were introduced, more copies of some models like the Walker Colts, have been made than were ever turned out originally. Two developments during the last 25 years have given the black powder sports a major push. Military and civilian organizations and clubs have been formed to duplicate those of a century or so ago, right down to the same uniforms and equipment. And then there have been new laws that make primitive muzzleloader hunting seasons legal in most states.

Military units commemorating the Indian Wars, the Revolution and the Civil War have created a demand for exact replicas of original uniforms, equipment, personal arms and even artillery. To meet the requirements of the Brigade of the American Revolution, for example, no nonperiod items are allowed. No digital watches, cigarette lighters, or zippers, and the barrel on your Brown Bess musket replica must be the correct 42 inches long, with all other features of the arm line-for-line correct when compared with an original. The result now is a quality assortment of authentic modern reproductions of historic muskets, rifles, fowling pieces and pistols.

Hunters have also done much to foster the availability of good quality and reasonably priced replicas. Ten years ago, few states had special seasons for muzzleloaders. Now, nearly all do. Many of the sportsmen attracted by these extra seasons were hunters first and black powder shooters a distant second. While they cared greatly about legal hunting, they gave less than a hoot about historic accuracy. What they wanted was a dependable modern muzzleloader.

From this demand came the Thompson Center Renegade, based on their earlier and more historically correct Hawken. The Renegade has a modern shotgun-style butt plate with no horns to poke you on recoil. It has adjustable sights so that a hunter can develop a load and then zero in his sights without files and a hammer. The Renegade Cougar has stainless fittings and lock parts to make it more durable and to look more like modern stainless models. The wood is quality American walnut.

Besides being used for hunting and reenacting battles from past wars, modern replica arms have rejuvenated a whole field of target and sport shooting. A few old-timers were still shooting originals in competition. But without the inexpensive replicas, there's no way the black powder sport could have achieved its present popularity.

Some stainless-steel muzzleloader revolvers and rifles have been built to modern designs and are intended specifically for competition. Others may become instant collectables. The reissued Colt 1860 Army revolver in blued steel and more expensive stainless only will be in production for a short period. Those who shoot it and care for it well may expect considerable appreciation. A quarter century from now, these few stainless models could be worth more than their original predecessors which fought the Civil War on both sides and helped open the West.

Demands by the buckskinners and others for accurate replicas like the Tennessee Mountain Squirrel Rifle in .32 caliber have caused many of these to be mass-produced. Both flintlock and percussion cap versions of these are available with extra locks and fittings so that one rifle can be converted to either ignition system.

Both factory-made and handcrafted Kentucky long rifles are popular. The one shown here is a handmade example by a hobbyist. Accurately styled modern rifles like this one, made with locks (LGR), barrels and fancy maple stock blanks, can cost upward of $5,000 when created

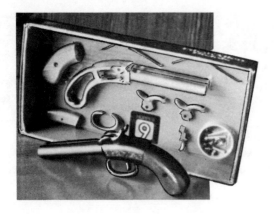

DOUBLE BARREL percussion Ethan Allen pocket pistol is available for under $100. It comes either as a parts kit or finished.

COMMEMORATIVE military unit, Ronald Plourde's Company of 4th Battalion Royal Artillery, fires cannons such as 3 pounder with South Bend Tube, Ashe carriage.

by top-ranking modern muzzle-loader gunsmiths. While this kind of expense can exceed the cost of an original, the buyer gets a safe rifle with a perfect bore capable of fine hunting or competition accuracy. Buyers also get a gun fitted to them so that it handles as no mass-produced arm ever will.

Besides historical working replicas, less well-known but interesting arms of the 19th century are being replicated. Finely crafted dueling pistols in both flint and percussion can double as target shooters from handgun enthusiasts.

Other manufacturers have introduced three copies of the early Ethan Allen pistols produced in New England in the 1840s. The pepperbox, so-called because its six rotating barrels looked something like a pepper mill, was one of the early muzzleloading repeaters. It was cheaper than Colt's revolvers at the time, and may also have gotten its name from its tendency to fire all six barrels at once and pepper anything in its path. A simple side-by-side double pistol and a single-shot target model are also in the Ethan Allen line,

selling for less than $100 in home assembly kits or available prefinished.

Time was when a percussion double shotgun cost less than $10 and you could find a good one in almost any antique shot. Those days are gone. That's not expensive, however, when compared to the prices of many modern doubles. What's more, muzzleloader shotguns shoot just as hard as modern breechloaders, and the second barrel of a double can be fired almost as quickly.

Cannon shooters have also gone the replica route. But they can rarely afford to go it alone. This may be a good thing, since it takes teamwork and correct procedures to shoot these monsters safely.

An International Muzzleloading Shooting Program has developed for firing everything from 16th-century Japanese matchlocks—a short length of clothesline ignites the charge—to modern replica percussion revolvers.

If the black powder sport is booming, and it is, it's because they don't build 'em like they used to. They build 'em better.

INDEX · VOLUME 11